THE LITERARY REVIEW

AN INTERNATIONAL JOURNAL OF CONTEMPORARY WRITING

LATE FALL 2012
VOL.55 / NO.4

ZONE 3
APSU
BOX 4565
CLARKSVILLE TN 37044

P9-CBM-336

All correspondence should be addressed to *The Literary Review*, USPS (025-646), 285 Madison Avenue, Madison, NJ 07940 USA. Telephone: (973) 443-8564. Email: info@theliteraryreview.org. Web: theliteraryreview.org. Periodical postage paid at Madison, NJ 07940 and at additional mailing offices. Subscription copies not received will be replaced without charge only if claimed within three months (six months outside US) from original date of mailing. Postmaster, send address changes to *The Literary Review*, 285 Madison Avenue, Madison, NJ 07940.

Manuscripts are read September through May. We only consider online submissions of poetry, fiction, and creative non-fiction. More information and guidelines at www.theliteraryreview.org.

Subscriptions: www.theliteraryreview.org
One year: $24 domestic, $32 international; Two year: $36 domestic, $45 international. Single issues: $8 domestic (international orders add $3 for postage and handling). Visa, MasterCard and American Express are accepted.

The Literary Review is a member of CLMP and CELJ. It is indexed in Humanities International Complete, Arts and Humanities Citation Index, MLA International Bibliography, Index of American Periodical Verse, Annual Index of Poetry in Periodicals, and the Literary Criticism Register. Microfilm is available from NA Publishing, Inc., P.O. Box 998, Ann Arbor, MI 48106. Full text electronic archives of *The Literary Review* are available through EBSCO Publishing by arrangement. The full text of *The Literary Review* is also available in the electronic versions of the Humanities Index from the H.W. Wilson Company, 950 University Avenue, Bronx, NY 10452. Selections from *The Literary Review* are available electronically through ProQuest LLC, 789 East Eisenhower Parkway, P.O. Box 1346, Ann Arbor, MI, 48106-1346. Visit proquest.com or call (800) 521-0600.

PRINTING BY THE PROLIFIC GROUP
150 WYATT ROAD, WINNIPEG, MB R2X 2X6, CANADA

COPYRIGHT ©2012
FAIRLEIGH DICKINSON UNIVERSITY
A QUARTERLY PUBLICATION
PRINTED IN CANADA

ISBN: 978-0-9860204-1-4

EBOOK ISBN: 978-0-9860204-2-1

Cover image © Mohamed Bourouissa

Courtesy the artist and kamel mennour, Paris

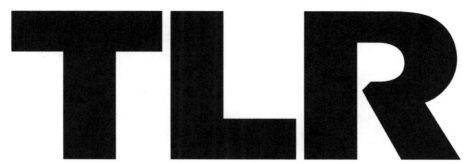

LOSS CONTROL
LATE FALL 2012

I first encountered the phrase "loss control" when one of my most talented former creative writing students announced that she'd taken her fine arts degree and secured a job at The Container Store, working in Loss Control—which meant she dressed incognito and followed suspicious characters around the store.

I adore, in particular the missing preposition, *of.* Loss of control is miles different than loss control, and that both phrases imply the total failure of anyone to do more than impede loss. Loss is inevitable, total control is unattainable, and total loss of control is deadly. Control is an abstraction and a grail. Humans are driven to maddening distraction, dangerous and untenable lengths, in pursuit of control. We don't ever get control, yet we hunt it. We hunt it because we hope it will give us some leverage over loss, which isn't a distraction but a kind of affliction.

The stories and poems our theme contained are vastly diverse: unhinged and crafty narrators dominate (as if the demonstration of control equaled actual control), people get lost in the desert, lost in their thoughts, disconnected from reality. Characters suffer complete loss of the senses, they murder, commit suicide, submit job applications, operate wobbly moral compasses and demonstrate robust appreciations of the absurd.

The loss of love, the loss of a loved one, the loss of our senses, of youth, the loss of merchandise—that broad spectrum of contingencies that keep us searching for solutions. And, as all good writers know, it's the searching that provides comfort. Especially if you can go incognito.

Minna Proctor

COVER ARTIST

MOHAMED BOUROUISSA
LE TÉLÉPHONE, 2007–2008
C-PRINT

When I received an email containing Mohamed Bourouissa's "Le Telephone" the image loaded on my screen from top to bottom in excruciatingly slow progress: first revealing that a group of boys existed, then exposing their eyes, followed by their mouths, and finally their bodies. Once their eyes were there, I began to wonder if the white boy was going to kiss or pummel the black boy. When his mouth filled in, I still was unsure. I waited, and waited, for his body to reveal his intentions, to let me know how the boy with the camera phone was sinning: was he capturing a sensual moment to text to his friends and spread homophobic gossip throughout the school, or if he was attempting to capture a moment of violence, sealing himself as the uninvolved onlooker, damning himself, as the willing crowd?

Looking at the photograph now, in it's full form, I'm still unsure. The image is from the series "Peripheries," thoroughout which Bourouissa, a French Algerian, toys with race, masculine energy, sexuality and the creation of otherness in French culture using what he calls "emotional geometry." Bourouissa uses real locations and intentionally stages subjects to appear not quite candid. This remove from reality creates a falsely safe distance from the emotions of the pieces which Bourouissa notes are communicated through the "interplay of eyes and power struggles." Often there are boys clustered in groups, one set of boys waiting, scoping out, sizing up the others. Gangs of boys crowded into a hallway, a circle of boys on a roof looking like they're ready for a group rumble, two boys facing off, ready to box. The tensions rely on an interaction not just between two people, but on the two people interacting in the context of a group. There is a kind of calm before the storm feeling, where the viewer knows that it may be minutes or hours or months before something happens, but that eruption is the inevitable conclusion.

These photos make my heart race. They sling me straight back into high school where violence and sexual risk was exciting, and then shoot me back into adulthood, where I know the danger these activities hold. The gap in time that these photographs represent, the memory of my own naiveté, is what gives the series its power. In an odd way, then, these photographs reassure me that the world is safe. At least, it is safer than it could be, if these boys lost control.

Jena Salon

LOSS CONTROL   LATE FALL 2012
VOL.55 / NO.4

Contents

Aubrie Marrin
In Case of Loss of Control

Red on red leaves on the road   nova blown   the season   I mean
the onslaught of

    How many times is there flare
    before it's over

Not to be confused with a supernova or a luminous red nova   there are
differences   *novae*   can you say cataclysmic   I think even they need
companions in the vacuum

    I am looking for extremely bright

        outbursts of light
        in shorter days

What about your mouth
lips teeth

    In spite of the violence

    I know these

You slouch and doom   bee-balm and the last of the season's bees
around you   how do I translate a shirt made of stars   also

the lighting is terrible

        but the lighting is always terrible.

There was a house   a porch in winter   but the ceiling the floor
the rooms dissolve   a world without

                threshold

and the weather comes

        right into you.

In Case of Sudden Danger

When startled, I am forced to move quickly.

There are reports on the bipedal behavior of octopuses   *Octopus marginatus*
coconut octopus tiptoeing along the ocean bottom   six of its arms
wrapped tightly around its body   the last two limbs
legs

      Off the island of Sulawesi   sixty to a hundred feet deep
      seeking out the sunken coconuts   drawing two halves
      around itself to hide

How does the moose prepare to live
among wolves

      to move

Weather systems whirl across the continent   I believe in motion   left to right
the words aren't speaking anymore   I've never stood at the edge
of the Grand Canyon

On Isle Royale, the packs of wolves hustle   the moose   hulking bull
tromps through snow packs

      On Isle Royale, sometimes it's cold enough that living tree trunks
      split in the night

A wolf track one long series of comet-shaped footprints

      The engine is running
      out of fuel

Should I leave out the pilot whales banked on the beach   bulbous heads
torpedoed bodies draped with wet white sheets   the common stranders
generally nomadic   each pod with its own pilot, its own discrete repertoire
of calls

      This behavior
      is significant

The moose think of eating fresh blue-bead lilies in the spring   we're flying
over the Great Lakes   holding this carcass with our large hands
we are two persons   pronouns   mouths
full of

     You let go first.

Donald Revell
Beyond Disappointment

Ascending through yellow broom and sluggish
Red-brown wasps, I found the new house.
In no way does it resemble the old.
Let there be no comparisons then,
No kisses before or shirtsleeves after.
I pull the comforter over my head,
And it is warm. The women spinning
In the next room weep as they spin.

Hence and farewell valediction: "life's journey."
It makes no sense. The children mock us with it.
A typewriter beneath the Christmas tree
Calls to the ice-caps. Illustrated monthlies
Burn in the wasps' burnt nest. It was
Such perfections made the sun to rise.

To Shakespeare

He made a statue of the east wind
Reconciled never too late, in
Silhouette, never too late as these
First days of March turn backwards,
Facing the full of winter in
Enduring love, full jollity
Of winter's face to reconcilement,
In silhouette.

             He did not forget
Who lost his life to remember it.
Step down. Do not be proud.
There is a double heart behind
The breast bone. Bare it. Beat it.
Begin to eat it in full view,
Who loves you every inch of the wind.
First days of March, lords of jollity.

The Cattle Were Lowing

It might also have been a sleigh ride.
Mozart's sister, a perfect oval and more
  than perfect incline,
Tucked into a blanket, laughs
For the first and last time in her life.

Genealogies tickle a little, and then a long
  pain afterwards—
Pain of connection, most awful
Pain of separation every Christmas.
Even angels find their armor
  burdensome then.

We rode across the snowy plain. The earth
Was mirror-glass ground into a fine powder.
Oh do not stop. Do not stop ever. I
Will give you a book of matches if . . .

There is the first of three dances still to consider,
And poverty, sole purpose of the wren.

Percival Everett
Little Faith

A spring-fed creek ran through the ranch, and so even in the harshest summer weeks there was a narrow lane of willows and green grass. Moose and elk browsed and left deep tracks in the muddy banks with the spent shells of the occasional poacher. Sam Innis had grown up there with his mother, his father having died in the war in Vietnam, a death that had come with no accompanying details. The woman had tenaciously clung onto her husband's dream, leasing out pasture, raising a few beefs and giving piano lessons to the ranch children in the wide valley. She turned down many offers on the place, saying that even imagining such a thing would be a betrayal. Love of the spread had been rubbed into Sam like so much salve, a barrier against whatever was out there in the world, a layer of peace, a perimeter of barbed wire. His mother held him close, not wanting to lose her only remaining family, but let the ranch, the land shape him. She let him go for his education and died while he was away at vet school. He had the old woman cremated and her ashes were mixed now into the dusty furrows, mud, and deep tracks of the life of that place. At dusk, when the owls and bats were whispering about, Sam would sit by the creek and watch the few trout rise to some hatch.

The desert rolled like always, constant, brown, ochre, and especially red in the distance. The pressure of people, the efforts of people had killed off much of the life, but none of the desert. His mother had said it: you can kill everything, you can tear it all up and build, you can pipe water to it, but the desert is the desert, more desert every day. It unfolded itself before him as he crested the ridge and started down the big sweeping curve of highway that would take him to the dirt trail to his place. The late morning sun was still behind him, but the shadows of the sage were beginning to shorten.

Sam and his wife were driving home from a memorial service. The oldest resident of the reservation had died at ninety-two. That was old for anyone, but especially for a Native man. Someone had told Sam that the life expectancy of an Indian male was forty-four. The Indian man who offered the statistic did so without the slightest show of bitterness or even fear. It's just a thing, he said. Ain't a good thing, ain't a bad thing, just a thing. Sam disagreed. The service had been at the Episcopal church. Sam didn't like churches.

Sam didn't know what the old man's death had been like. Apparently he was walking one minute and not the next. Sam hadn't known Old Dave Wednesday very well, for only a few years, but once, while Sam was out examining the horses at the tribal ranch, the two sat together on mustard-studded hillside.

I am an old man, Dave said.

I suppose, Sam agreed. How old are you exactly?

Ninety.

That's old. My mother didn't live to be near that old.

They had hiked up the fairly steep hill to look down at the ranch. Dave was telling him how the tribe planned to bring water down-mountain via an old-fashioned drainage ditch.

Dave pointed at the hills with an open, shaky hand. From over there. Them surveyors came and looked and said it was possible. Said we need some engineers. And all of them want to get paid money. They want to get paid money for everything. Even for telling us how much it will cost.

Sam nodded.

Dave rubbed his knees. I'm glad to be sitting. I can't walk like I used to.

None of us can, Sam said.

I will die soon.

Sam was not so comfortable with this talk, but he said, We all die. He hated his platitude.

So, I'm told. And there is nothing wrong with it, though I'm not sure I believe it. If you do it right, then you don't have to do it again.

They sat silent for a bit longer. Sam looked at the horses in the pasture below and then over at the yellow hills where the water would come from. Measure twice, cut once, he said.

Dave laughed. Then he laughed again, at something else.

What is it? Sam asked.

Us, the old man said. We are Sam and Dave. We are soul men. He laughed again, louder.

Sam brought the pickup to a stop on the gravel next to the house. He and Sophie sat there for a few seconds and let the ticking of the killed engine settle into silence. They stared ahead at the fenced pasture and the flowering willows far off along the creek. His mother had always been fond of the *salix exigua*, the coyote willow, almost as fond of them as the elk. A colt pranced around his mother.

You okay? Sophie asked.

Sam looked at her.

About having been in a church.

Sam chuckled. He did not like churches. Yes, I'm okay. Let's get changed so we can take care of these beasts.

Zip, the border collie, greeted them at the door and followed them into the house through the kitchen. Sophie stopped at the counter to check the phone messages. Sam walked upstairs, peeled off his jacket and undid the knot of his tie. He sat on the bed and kicked off his shoes.

These shoes hurt my feet, he said as Sophie entered.

You always say that.

It's always true. You should bury me in them. That way you'll know I won't be doing any ghostly walking.

I was looking forward to your ghostly walking.

You are a sweet-talker, aren't you?

Yes, I am. She unhooked her the back of her dress and let it slide down her body to the floor.

All right. And you're a tease.

Yes, I am.

Come here, Missy. He reached for her hand.

You know I love it when you talk cowboy.

Do you now? Come here.

Me?

Yes, you, ma'am.

He stood and held her, kissed her.

The house shifted, it seemed. Then the whole structure shook, swayed as if riding a wave. They clung to each other. There was a crash downstairs. The little electric clock bounced off of Sam's nightstand. And then it was over and everything was quiet for a brief moment. The mules brayed and the horses called out. Then Zip started barking.

Wow. Sophie dropped to a knee and comforted the dog. Earthquake?

I'm guessing so.

Sam slipped back into his dress shoes, did not tie the laces and headed for the stairs. Sophie grabbed her robe and pulled it on as she followed him down. Sam wondered if there would be another tremor. At the bottom he could see that the framed picture of his mother had fallen, but the glass had cracked only. Other pictures were askew, but nothing seemed to be broken. They stepped into the mudroom and changed into their boots, then walked out the kitchen door. The world didn't appear any different. The sky was cloudless. The hills were still standing at their same heights in the distance. Zip ran in tight circles. The horses were stirred up. The skittish roan mare was kicking her stall wall in the near barn. A loose barn door that Sam had been meaning to repair for weeks now lay flat in the dust.

You go settle down the horses, Sam said. I'll check the propane.

Sam watched Sophie move off. She stopped to say something soft to the little donkey in the paddock just outside the barn. Zip stayed with Sam. She always stayed with Sam. He went to the cabinet on the exterior wall next to the back door and grabbed a pipe wrench and a spray bottle filled with soapy water. The large green propane tank was thirty yards from the house. It looked fine, but of course that meant nothing. He listened as he looked at the gauge and felt and sniffed around the joints. He sprayed the connections and saw no bubbles. The line to the house was underground; there was no checking that. He walked back to the house and into the kitchen. He pushed the stove away from the wall a bit and sprayed the line. All good. In the cellar he checked the furnace. The pilot was surprisingly still lit. No leaks. Same with the water heater. Sophie was in the kitchen when he came back up.

Everything all right? She asked.

No problems.

I can't believe we had an earthquake. She sat at the table. I didn't even know we had a fault.

You don't, Sam said.

Who's the sweet-talker?

The barns?

Just that door. Horses are scared.

Horses are always scared. They'll be fine in ten minutes. Sam set the spray bottle on the table. I guess we should turn on the radio.

They sat in the kitchen, drank tea, and listened to the local station. There had in fact been a quake—the magnitude of which had not been determined—a surprise to everyone and a source for incessant chatter. There was little to report in the way of damage and they quickly grew tired of people calling in to repeat the experience of the previous caller. Broken canned goods, cracked washer drums, ruined china sets. One woman called to say that in the minutes right before the quake her chickens, to a hen, had each laid an egg.

And how does she know that? Sophie laughed.

The rooster told her, Sam said. He looked out the window. I figure the office phone will start ringing soon. Now that everybody has figured out they're all right, they'll start seeing stuff wrong with their animals.

The phone rang.

Sam picked up.

It was Norma Snow from north of town. She was a new transplant, from California to live the quiet life. I want to buy a horse and I need a vet check, she said.

What'd you think of the quake? Sam asked.

That was hardly a quake, the woman said.

I guess not for you.

There's this beautiful leopard appaloosa down near Randy Gap. Can you meet me there this afternoon? Two?

Sam looked at the clock. It was twelve-thirty. Two-thirty?

That's good.

I'll meet you at the flashing light at two-thirty.

He hung up.

Didn't sound like an emergency, Sophie said.

City woman wants a horse, Sam said. Everybody ought to have a horse. And the lucky ones of us can have mules.

You and your mules.

I'm supposed to look at Watson's mare at one and that's one-thirty. That won't take long and that's on the way to the Gap.

What about lunch?

I'll take an apple with me.

Sophie made a disapproving face.

Two apples.

Just make sure you don't feed one to a horse.

Yes, ma'am.

Leave her alone. Treat her like a horse.

Sam walked out of the house and to his work truck, where he inspected his vet pack. It was his habit. He restocked every time he returned home and checked his supplies always before setting out. The sky remained clear, if a little cool, but heat was on the way. Zip hopped into the truck before him.

He drove the unused back roads to the ranch of Wes Watson. The back way was actually faster, but rough on the suspension, the truck's and his. He looked at Zip as they bounced along. Probably not the best thing for my prostate, he said to her. The mare he was seeing he'd seen before for vaccinations and once for a hoof problem. Now Wes wanted to breed her.

Wes met him at his truck. Greetings.

Greetings to you, Sam laughed.

I thought it seemed like a pleasant way to, to . . . .

Greet someone? Sam offered.

More or less.

So, you want to breed the paint. You think she's in season?

You're here to tell me.

Live cover?

Nope. Sperm's on the way.

Sam nodded. He followed Wes into the barn. The quarter horse was standing calmly, already cross-tied in a washstand and backed up against a rail. Sam looked at her while he pulled on his glove. Well, her tail's up, isn't it.

Her tail's always up, Wes said.

Sam gave the horse's neck a gentle stroke and moved his hand down to her flank. He slowly inserted his gloved hand into the animal's vagina. She took a step, but stayed calm. He could see she was in estrus before he was inside. He felt around, shook his head.

What is it? Wes asked.

We might have a problem, Sam said. He felt around more. I think she's got a hematoma.

Is that bad?

Sam carefully removed his arm and hand. No, not bad. But she won't be getting knocked up for a while. She's going to have to cycle a few times before this resolves itself. Won't affect her fertility. Shouldn't, anyway. We'll keep an eye on her.

How do you know it's not a tumor?

The other ovary feels normal. If it was a tumor, the other would probably be smaller than normal. Plus, she's not acting all crazy with hormones. I'm going to take some blood to be sure.

All right. That's disappointing.

Sam flexed his hand, rolled down his shirtsleeve. She sure is a pretty horse, I'll give you that. I see why you want to breed her.

She's a looker. Even-tempered, too.

They walked back to Sam's truck. Zip lay in the vehicle's shadow.

So, did you feel the shaker? Wes asked.

Oh yeah.

We hardly did. The wind chimes on the porch shook. That was about it. So, where you headed from here?

Down to Randy Gap. Vet check.

Wes nodded and kicked at the dirt. So, I just leave her alone, that's it? Wes asked about the horse.

Leave her alone. Treat her like a horse. Sam opened a cabinet of the pack on the back of his pickup, pulled out a syringe kit and some vials. I'll get me a little bit of blood and I'll be on my way.

You know, you're okay, Wes said.

Sam looked at him. How's that?

You know, being a black vet way out here. I have to admit to you, I had my doubts.

About what exactly?

Whether you'd make it.

You mean fit in?

I guess that's what I mean, yeah.

Wes, I grew up here. Grade school. High school. I've never fit in. I probably will never fit in. I accept that.

Wes's face was now blank as if he'd entered some territory he didn't recognize. He was just a degree away from cocking his head like a confused hound.

Sam said, But thanks, Wes. I'm glad you think I'm okay.

That's all I was saying.

I know, Wes.

Randy Gap, eh? Bad medicine down there.

That what folks in the tribe say?

No, that's what I say. You don't have to be no Indian to spot it.

I suppose that's right.

Sam left Wes there in the sun, walked back into the barn to collect blood from the paint mare.

Randy Gap was the confluence of two draws and two roads and the place had nothing to do with anyone named Randy or Randolph. It had been so named because supposedly every time old-timers drove cattle through there the bulls would get crazy horny and slow everything down. Now it was the weather in the gap that slowed everything down, snow and rain and wind seemed to concentrate on the area. It was windy when Sam found Norma Snow waiting there leaning against her Subaru. He crunched to a halt on the gravel roadside.

Hey, Norma.

Doc.

So, you want to buy yourself a new horse.

It's not far, she said. Couple of miles.

I'll follow you. He watched the woman walk back to her car. She was his age, but she looked younger. Or maybe it was that he looked older. What was forty-four supposed to look like?

He trailed her to a dirt road and then a half-mile in to a trailer home surrounded by pipe corrals and paddocks. Horses stood in most of the enclosures, some clean, some not. He'd seen places like this before and there was little good about them. He parked behind Norma and got out. He left Zip in the truck.

A sandy-haired teenage boy came from the trailer. He wore a tight tee shirt that said One in the Oven with a downward-pointing arrow. He tossed his cigarette butt into the dirt and didn't bother to step on it.

Well, here I am, Norma said.

I'll get him, the kid said without expression.

Warm, Sam said, referring to the boy's greeting.

The teenager came back with a fifteen-hand appaloosa gelding with a nicely defined blanket on his rump. The horse was clean and freshly shod.

Isn't he beautiful? Norma was not playing the role of the cool buyer. She stepped back and looked at the horse.

Sam circled the animal. Nice markings, all right, he said. But that's not why I'm here, is it? He reached out to shake the kid's hand. I'm Sam Innis, the vet.

The boy shook his hand. Jake.

Sam let go of the boy's limp mitt. Let's take a look at him. Is there anything you want to tell us?

The boy shook his head. I don't know anything. They come in, we sell them. This one eats everything we put down, I can tell you that.

You mind trotting him over there about twenty yards and then back to me? Sam watched as the kid led the horse away. They kicked up dust. Sam rubbed his chin and studied the animal. As they were coming back he said, He's a little wide in the chest. See how he paddles? Like he's swimming.

Is that bad? Norma asked.

Better than being too narrow and knocking his feet together. He won't be much good jumping anything. He asked the boy to repeat the trot away and back. He's loose in the caboose like an Arabian. Norma, his legs are everywhere. What do you want to do with him?

Ride trails, that's all.

Sam nodded. He might be okay. I can see why you like him. He's pretty. Being wide is a good thing for your comfort. Well, let's take a closer look. He's not exactly wide through the stifles. Sam caught himself. He didn't want to be too negative. After all, Norma liked the horse.

The winded boy came back with the horse and stood quietly. Sam measured the circumference of the leg just below the knee. Good bone. He grabbed the knee. He's just a little buck-kneed.

Norma came close and looked with Sam.

Sam looked at Norma. He's got a beautiful coat. Flies don't seem to bother him. Sam looked at the horse's eyes and then at the boy. Just how much bute did you give him?

A little, the boy admitted, caught off guard.

What is it? Norma asked.

Will he lunge? Sam asked.

Yeah, Jake said.

Sam took the lead rope from the boy and got the horse trotting counterclockwise around him. He stopped him and picked up his left forefoot.

What is it? Norma asked.

They gave the horse a drug for pain. He's got some navicular issues. I mean, Norma, you can live with all the problems I'm finding, I'm sure. Corrective shoes will help his heels, but he won't be much good for long or strenuous rides. What are they asking for him?

Three grand, Jake said.

Sam smiled. I wouldn't pay more than eight hundred.

You're crazy, the kid said. He was red in the face.

I've been told that, Sam said. Norma, I can keep checking him, but it won't get better.

This horse is sound, the kid snapped.

Sam nodded.

I guess I'll pass, Norma said to Jake.

So, that's it? the boy grunted.

Thanks for showing him to me, Norma said.

Yeah, right. He muttered something to himself as he walked the horse away.

Sam walked with Norma back to her car.

I think he's pissed, she said.

He was trying to rip you off. Maybe not the kid, but the guy he works for. Healthy horses are expensive enough to take care of.

Thanks, Doc.

Sam felt bad. Norma had had high hopes for the animal, was a little bit in love with him. He watched her fall in behind the wheel of her car, start it, and have a bit of trouble getting turned around.

Sam climbed into his own truck and laughed when he had the same difficult time getting himself about-faced. He drove home.

Sophie answered the ringing phone as Sam stepped into the kitchen. He sat on the bench in the mudroom and untied the laces on his boots.

We're fine, Sophie said. What about you? That's good. Oh, I see. Well, he just walked in. She handed the phone to Sam. It's the sheriff.

Dale, Sam said.

You okay over there? Any damage? the sheriff asked.

Nothing. What's up?

I'd like you to come out here and give us a hand. We've got a lost little girl up next to the reservation. Up in the Creeks.

How long has she been lost?

About six hours. I'm down at the little store at the flashing light. Only place I can get a signal on my damn phone.

Can you get in touch with Eddie over there? Sam asked.

Yes.

Have Eddie get me a horse ready. That way I won't have to waste time getting one loaded into a trailer here.

All right, you got it. I've got six men out now, four on horseback, two on foot. Of course the only thing the quake damaged in the whole fucking county was the helicopter. We're waiting on one to come from Casper. Duncan's flying his Beechcraft around.

Where are you exactly?

You'll see us. Just take the road on through to the far side of the rez. Just past the big dip.

All right.

Oh, and Sam.

Yes?

The girl is deaf.

He's got a beautiful coat. Flies don't seem to bother him. Sam looked at the horse's eyes and then at the boy. Just how much bute did you give him?

I'm on my way. Be there in less than an hour. He hung up.

Sophie was standing close. What?

Little deaf girl is lost out in the Owl Creeks.

That's got to be Sadie White Feather's girl.

Dale didn't tell me her name.

She's so tiny.

When Sam came back from the washroom off the kitchen, Sophie handed him a knapsack.

Water, she said. Some fruit and some cookies. The cookies of course are for the child.

Yes, ma'am. I'm going to grab my chaps from the tack shed. Might have to pop some brush.

He gave her a kiss and stepped outside, called for Zip.

*

The sheriff had set up a staging area at the head of a little-used trail. It was two hundred square miles of barren, desolate, arid hills, full of worthless ore and seasonal creeks that could flood in a blink. The county-reservation line was somewhere around there, but no one knew for sure and no one really cared. Sam and Zip fell out of the truck and walked to the sheriff. He was trying to talk with someone on a handheld radio. Sadie White Feather was sitting on a picnic folding chair a few yards away. She did not look up at the sound of Sam's approach.

Dale, Sam said.

I'm glad you're here. These damn radios work for shit in these hills. I don't know where the fuck anybody is.

Sam looked at the hills. Old Dave Wednesday would never set foot in them, called them haunted, bad medicine. Sam had actually liked the place, had ridden there once.

The tribal police put me in charge. Mainly because I'm suppose to have a helicopter. But I don't. Anyway, the whole tribal force, all three of them, are out there looking.

Okay.

Along with my two deputies and that new ranger, Epps.

What exactly is the situation?

Dale glanced over at Sadie White Feather. He motioned for Sam to follow him away a few paces. Girl's name is Penny. She went and wandered off away from the family's camp and just never came back. She was here with her mother, aunt, uncle, and grandmother. Her uncle's a tribal cop; he's out looking. The aunt and grandma went to find the father.

Sam nodded. They see anybody else around?

No. Did I mention that the radio reception is crappy in these damn hills? Cell phones are worse.

You mentioned it. Any sign yet?

Nothing reported.

Sam stepped over to look at the map the sheriff had spread out on the hood of his rig. It was held down from the wind by rocks. Circles had been drawn and x's were placed in spots.

She's only nine, Sam. How much ground could she have covered?

A lot, Sam said. And these canyons are just crazy. You could pass by the same wash three times and never know it. Mind if I talk to Sadie?

Be my guest.

Zip had already made it over to the woman and pushed up under her hand. Sadie was absently patting the dog's head.

Sadie, Sam said.

The woman looked up.

It's me, Sam Innis. You know my wife, Sophie.

Sadie nodded.

I'm going to go out and help look for Penny. Sam took a knee, faced the direction she faced, and studied the same empty space. But I need to ask you a few questions. You've been asked a bunch, I know, but a couple more, okay? They tell me Penny's nine.

Nine and a half.

Exactly where and when did you last see her?

She was playing over by those yellow mounds. She pointed with an open hand. She was throwing rocks. She glanced over at me and I signed for her to stop throwing rocks, but she pretended not to hear. We say hear even though she can't.

I understand.

Anyway, she kept on throwing rocks. My sister said to just let her throw rocks, she wasn't hurting nothing. I started cooking breakfast. I was making some chokecherry gravy. When I looked back over there, I didn't see her. I didn't think anything of it, then and I went back to cooking. Then I got to thinking about how she can't hear snakes and so I went on over and looked for her. I looked all over and then my sister and her husband started looking and we couldn't find her. I guess that was about eight-thirty, maybe nine.

Is she completely deaf?

Yes.

Can you show me how to sign her name?

You just put one finger to your forehead and moved it out. Like this. It's kind of a joke. We call her One Cent. You know, a penny is one cent.

Like this? Sam repeated the motion.

The woman nodded. She might laugh at you.

How do I say friend?

Sadie showed him. Crossed fingers this way and that.

Got it. And that's about all my old head can hold. And is Penny left- or right-handed?

Right. She does some things with her left. She brushes her teeth with her left hand. I've tried and I can't do it.

I know you were making breakfast, but did she eat anything this morning?

Nothing.

Did she drink water?

She always drinks a lot of water. Oh, she had a juice box, too.

Good, that's a good thing. What about her shoes? What kind of shoes is she wearing?

Sneakers, Sadie said. You know, those kind the kids love with the heels that light up when they take a step. She loves them. They're a little small on her. I guess that doesn't matter.

It matters and it helps to know, Sam said. Everything matters. Tell me, Sadie, is Penny a smart girl?

All A's in school. She's very, very smart. She knows the capitols of all the states.

How much does she weigh?

Not much. I don't know. She's little. Fifty pounds? Not even.

Thanks, Sadie. We're going to find her, okay? That was what Sam said, because that's what one always said in those situations. He'd been a tracker for a long time and he'd never once set out actually believing he would find anyone, but he always said he would.

Sam walked back to the sheriff.

You need an article of clothing for your dog? Dale asked.

She's not a scent dog. She can't smell bacon cooking. But any dog is better than three men.

The roan over there is what Eddie drove over for you. He's driving the highway, just in case she makes her way, or . . . you know. And here's a radio, for all the good it will do you. Just try it periodically. It might work.

Dale's radio awoke with static and he stepped away, trying to find a stronger signal. Sam looked at the map again, then walked over to where Sadie had last seen the child throwing rocks. He picked up a few stones and hurled them at a boulder. Not far from the yellow formation was a narrow wash between waist-high walls. Not so intriguing for an adult, Sam thought, but probably irresistible for a child. The ground there had been pretty well trampled by men's boots and shod horses and then it became rocky. He decided he'd follow the wash.

He walked back to the roan, gave him a rub on the neck. He knew the horse, had treated him a couple of times. He of course realized that the horse did not remember him. He tightened the cinch of the synthetic saddle. The horse was a short, sturdy, big-butted quarter horse, good for breaking through growth. He mounted, whistled for Zip, and rode on.

Into the ravine. The walls were saddle high until the rocks opened up, spread away from the wash as it widened and joined another drainage. He saw where a couple of riders had gone on north. He veered down and around a steep hill and rode on a mile or so. He checked his radio and already it was useless. These hills were full of something magnetic, he figured, or it was just spirits and Old Dave had been right. He messed with the squelch on the radio and was just able to hear Dale swearing at the other end.

He rode on slowly, looking ahead and scouting the distance and casting a glance down to study the ground and brush. He looked for something, anything, the tiniest thing out of the ordinary, a drag, a broken stick, even an animal acting strange. The ground was baked hard with a fine layer of loose sand that the wind played with. He dismounted and looked closely at the surface, moved his sight up slowly, squinted. He stared and stared. A lopsided creosote bush caught his eye. He led the horse to it. It was snapped off about a foot off the ground. It was a fairly fresh break. Anything could have caused the damage; he knew that. Still it was something. He combed the ground around and near the bush. Then, in a spot protected from the wind, he thought he saw some transfer of soil over pebbles and just beyond that some indentations where pebbles had rested. Hardly a definite sign, but he decided to view it as transfer and that gave him at least direction. He looked up and observed the clouds and sky to the east. Back in the saddle, he watched Zip sniff around some coyote scat. She left it in short order and heeled to the roan.

Sam rode up to a bit of high ground and looked over the terrain. He had come to an expanse of flat ground. Far off to the north he could make out the dust of a couple of riders, but he couldn't tell which way they were going. Above him a hawk circled high. There was an outcropping to the east, the direction he'd chosen. There was nothing between him and the rocks and so he rode toward the formation, the light sinking behind him.

The sun was a couple of hours from setting and was already giving the west-facing rocks an eerie bronze shimmer. The wind picked up and blew sand in sheets into his back. There would be no trail, human or otherwise. He stopped and examined a couple of odd spots anyway, thought one might have been where a small person had taken a knee to rest. He was reaching and recalled how easy it was for a man to see what he wanted to see.

The outcropping was surprisingly larger than it had seemed from a distance. There was plenty of space between boulders for a large person to wander into and get lost. The wind was whipping now and in these rocks it was bouncing and twisting in all directions. The temperature was quickly dropping. He considered letting the horse stand on a dropped rein, but because of the wind tied up to some sage instead. He tried the radio. Nothing. He looked at the sky, listened for a plane or helicopter. There was nothing.

Sam left the horse and with Zip wended his way into the formation of rocks. They came out into a bowl, the floor of which was an expanse of flat rock. On the table of rock were a considerable number of rattlesnakes basking in the last rays of the day's sun, trying to collect all the warmth they could from the stone. In the middle of the flat area, in the middle of the snakes, was a washtub-shaped rock, and on it sat a little girl. Sam called out and immediately realized the futility in that. He told Zip to stay, said it twice. His actions now were very important. If he startled the child she might panic and move into the snakes. He didn't know if she was aware of the snakes; he had to assume she was not. His back was to the west and so he would be in silhouette. What could be scarier that a hulking shadow at dusk? Also, with his back to the west he couldn't use his watch crystal or anything else to reflect the sun to get the girl's attention. He moved left, moved to put himself somewhere else in relation to the sun. He could see that the child's eyes were open, but she stared blankly at the rocks thirty or so feet in front of her. He was losing the day, the light. It was colder still. He reached down and scraped together a handful of small stones. He repeated his command back to Zip to stay. He walked into the snakes, wishing he had worn taller boots. His Wellingtons came up only to mid-calf.

He pitched a pebble at the girl. It landed without effect near her sneakered heels. He tossed another and it skittered across the plane of rock in front of her and this time she saw it. She turned and looked at Sam. He froze. Stepping as he was through the snakes, he was certain that his posture, his body language would be difficult for her to read. He must have looked strange. He could see fear coming over her face. He put his hands up and signed friend to her. Whether he was doing it correctly, he didn't know. The fact that he was signing at all at least let her know that he knew something about her. He put his hands out, palms down, as if to tell her to relax. He then pointed to the snakes. It was unclear whether she was seeing them for the first time, but she pulled her feet up onto the rock and held her knees to her chest. Good, Sam said, but didn't know how to sign that, so he nodded. Perhaps she could read lips and then he wondered how much lip he showed under his bush of a mustache. He signed friend again. He looked back to see if Zip was obeying his last command and she was. Penny was wearing only a tee shirt and sweatpants. She was no doubt feeling the cold or would be very soon. A snake rattled near Sam. The sound echoed off the rocks. He looked around and tried to locate the agitated animal. Zip barked. Sam again gestured to the child to remain calm. He took another step, watched as his boot landed between two rattlers, either one just inches away. He was about twelve feet from Penny when a three-foot long snake uncoiled and struck his boot. If the animal had rattled first he might not have been so startled, but he was and so took an awkward step and lost his balance. He put out a hand and caught himself. A small snake found his hand and bit it. He stood up and the snake fell off. He looked at the bite, not believing it. He looked back at Zip, saw she was concerned, and reminded her to stay. He looked at the girl, at all of the snakes, at his hand. Fuck, he said, fuck, fuck, fuck. He was glad the girl was deaf. Fuck. He told himself to calm down, to breathe slower, evenly. The bite pushed him on and in two steps he was on the little island with Penny.

They sat there and stared straight ahead. Neither cast a glance at the other. Well, young lady, Sam said, but obviously to himself, What we have here is two gallons of shit in a one-gallon bucket. He looked at his hand; there was little blood. I'll bet you're glad the big man has come to rescue you. He let out a nervous laugh, then sighed out a long breath, trying to slow his panic, his heart rate. He tapped the child on the shoulder and gestured that he wanted her to climb onto his back. He pointed at her and then at his back. He held out his unbitten hand and smiled. She leaned over and looked at his injured hand. He showed it to her. Yeah, he got me. I wish the fact that he was little meant something good, but it doesn't. She reached out and touched the hand, her fingers cool against his skin, small, light.

Sam turned his back slightly to her and patted his shoulder. The girl understood, put her arms around his neck, and climbed on. He stood, found her remarkably light, weightless. His hand hurt and he thought he could feel it swelling. So, much for any hope that it was a dry bite. He walked less gingerly on the way back, feeling a new sense of urgency, both for the girl and for himself, also recognizing that his too-careful pace had been the reason for his bite. He also harbored the notion that like lightning the snakes would not strike twice. That notion turned out to be incorrect. After successfully kicking away a couple of snakes, a large one that he did not see struck and latched onto his calf just below his knee. He reached down, grabbed the snake and hurled it away. The bite hurt like hell. Zip was barking and bouncing, but still she stayed.

Clear of the snakes, Sam gently put down the child and collapsed to his knees, mainly in disbelief. He was swelling at both bites and he either felt or imagined some tingling in his mouth. He felt weak. He was certainly dizzy. He stood and guided the girl back through the maze of boulders to the horse. He tried the radio. Static. Dusk was on now and everything was indistinct. An owl hooted somewhere. The air was much colder. Or was it chills?

By his reckoning he was six or seven miles from where he had left the sheriff. A voice scratched through the radio. He pressed the talk button. Say again. This is Innis. Nothing. In case you can hear me, I have little Penny with me. Come in. I repeat, the child is safe, unharmed, and with me. However, I have managed to get myself bitten twice by rattlers. I'm about six miles southeast of the staging area. Be advised, need help. Do you read? Static. Maybe they heard me, he said to the girl. He pointed to his ear.

He opened his knapsack that he'd tied to the saddle and pulled out his first aid kit. Never leave home without a snakebite kit, kid. In fact, he'd never used a kit or treated a human for a bite. Bites to horses were rare and horses were so big that they usually just got a little sick and got better. Considering how long it had taken him to get to the kit, it seemed a lot like closing the barn door after whatever was already out.

If only he'd been bitten only once, he'd probably be okay because of his size. But two bites, that was a different matter. Two bites at distant sites. He addressed the bite on his leg since it was more recent and because the snake had been bigger. He cut his pant leg with his pocketknife and ripped it up to his knee. He then swabbed the area of the bite with an antiseptic pad. He fumbled with the sterile blade, nearly dropped it when he pulled it from the plastic sleeve. He sliced through the two fang holes and used the extractor to draw out what blood and poison he could. He hurt like hell while he did it. For some reason, swearing helped and so he did, pleased at least that the child could not hear him. He wondered if she could swear in sign language. He finished, looked at his hand. He had reservations about using the same blade again on his hand. He decided that he should not. Penny watched. He stopped and listened. The world seemed quieter with her there.

Sam studied the darkening landscape. He wished he had a flare gun, then laughed at himself. He could also wish that he could teleport them back in time. If we had some ham we could have ham and eggs if we had some eggs, he said. He tried the radio again. Dale's voice scratched through.

Dale, he said.

Sam? Night air seems to help the signal.

Dale, I found her. I have her here with me.

Everybody, he found her, Dale said to others. There was cheering in the background.

She's okay, unhurt. I'm about six or so miles east and a little south of you. I wish I could be more precise.

Copy that.

Dale, I've been bitten twice by rattlers.

Jesus, Sam. How bad?

I don't know. We're going to start back. I have a flashlight burning. I'll be sticking to flat ground. Come out and try to meet us.

Roger that. We'll find you.

Leaving now.

We'll find you, Dale repeated.

Sam took off his jacket and put it around Penny. He mounted and then pulled her up into the saddle in front of him. He cantered for a while, but the horse felt uneven. The girl was too small to add enough weight to be a problem. He stopped, got down, and looked at the horse's feet. The animal had a quarter crack on his left forefoot. He was hurting. If the animal came up lame, they'd be in a real fix, he thought. He put Penny back in the saddle and led the horse, walking as briskly as he could. His mouth was surely tingling now. The swelling at both sites was now undeniable. He was sweating and his mouth was wet with saliva. He spat and spat again. The sweating made him cold and then there were the chills. He did not yet feel nauseated, but he knew that was coming. He wished the girl could hear and speak, because he needed the distraction of conversation to keep himself together. He wanted to lie down, fold up, and go to sleep. Zip stayed extra close, sensing trouble. I'll be all right, girl, he said to the dog. You just keep me awake.

It was dark now. The nausea was beginning. The dizziness was more profound. He was glad he wasn't in the saddle. He'd probably slide right off. He was worried about a lot of things now. Walking in a straight line is hard to do, he remembered, and without a distant visual point of reference it was near impossible. Given his disorientation there would be no reckoning by the stars, even if he could do it all. The last thing he needed was to lead them off into the wilderness away from where they were expected to be. He stopped the horse and brought the girl down. He pushed down in the air with his palms, trying to say that they would wait there. He pulled some sagebrush together into a pile and in short order she was helping. He broke off some creosote branches and started a fire. There was a lot of smoke at first, chasing him the way smoke often does. It stung his eyes. He then imagined that the burning sage might cleanse him. He fanned it over his body as he'd seen Old Dave and other Natives do on so many occasions. He laughed at himself; he was hardly a believer in anything. He looked to find the child doing the same thing with the smoke. He pushed at the flames and watched it catch better.

He put on more branches. The fire was large now, he thought, easy to spot from the sky or a distance. It warmed them, but it did nothing to stop his chills. He thought he heard a plane buzzing someplace. Penny took his hand, his bitten hand into her small grasp. He looked at her, felt himself drifting. He watched the flames, advancing, retreating, dancing, hypnotic the way flames always are. There was Dave Wednesday, younger than he had ever been while Sam knew him, sitting in front of a fireplace in a cabin.

You're thinking you're having a vision, aren't you? Dave said.

Pretty much. As offensive as that must sound to you.

Snake-bit?

Afraid so.

Dave offered Sam a mug of coffee. That stuff is real strong, will keep you awake for days and days. You're not a spiritual person, are you?

That's an understatement.

Yet, here you are, hallucinating stereotypes. You don't have to be spiritual. I don't know what that means anyway. So, here you are, he repeated.

Pretty much. Sam drank some of the coffee. It was actually rather weak, though it was too hot to even sip. So, how do I handle these bites?

You're the doctor.

I forgot. The earthquake sort of scared me. You were dead, so you didn't feel it. It was the surprise more than anything.

I felt it. Where do you think they buried me? Where are those bites? Dave asked.

One's on the back of my leg and on this hand. Little snake bit me here. He held up his hand. This is the one I'm worried about. You know, they say the little ones have more potent venom.

Could be.

Dave held Sam's hand and looked closely at it. Yes, it looks like a snake bit you. Did you get his name?

Rattler.

That's not good. I've seen a fair share of bites in my time. Seen a fair share of people dropped down into the soil because of bites that looked just like that one. I daresay the soil is fat with the corpses of people with bites like that one. Does that make you nervous?

I can't say that it makes me happy to hear it.

I have a joke for you. How many Indians does it take to screw in a light bulb?

I don't know, how many?

None. The Indians just stand still while the white man does the screwing. Dave laughed. Here's another. How many blacks does it take to screw in a light bulb?

Go ahead.

Probably one, but you can't do it with your hands shackled to your waist. And do you know what the real punch line is?

No.

Rattlesnake. Come with me, Dave said. And he led Sam into a house and then out through the back door onto a big porch where some men were shooting dice.

It's your turn, someone said and put the dice in Sam's hand. Sam tossed the dice, and the number five came up. The point is seven, someone shouted. What are we playing for? another said. The pot had some bills in it, not more that twenty dollars. A tall man had a pistol stuck into his belt.

Let's play for the pistol, Sam said.

The tall man put the pistol into the pot. Why do you want it? he asked.

I don't think anybody should have it, Sam said. If I win it, I'm going to throw it into the pit under the outhouse.

The tall man shrugged.

And what do I get if you lose? the tall man asked. What about your gold tooth? He pointed at Sam's mouth.

Sam didn't know he had a gold tooth. He nodded in agreement.

He threw down the dice. Snake-eyes.

He turned to Dave and said, Come on with me. Dave followed Sam to the bank of a dry streambed about thirty yards from the house. He reached into his pocket and pulled out a vise-grip. Do it fast, he said and opened his mouth.

I'm not going to pull your tooth, Dave said.

Listen, I'm not crazy about it either, but I lost.

Dave held the pliers in his shaky hand. He reached into Sam's mouth. I don't like this.

Just do it fast.

Dave did it. Sam looked at the tooth and it wasn't gold. Dave looked at it too and then back into Sam's bloody mouth. Oops, he said.

Sam put his handkerchief into his mouth and bit down on it. They walked back to the house without speaking. Sam put the tooth in the tall man's hand.

The man looked disappointedly at the white tooth.

We're not going back to do it again, Sam said. That's the tooth you get.

Dave looked at the man and said, Rattlesnake.

When Sam opened his eyes, he was sitting in front of the sage fire with Penny. The fire had not died down at all. He pushed some more sticks into the flames. He felt the warmth of it and realized that his chills were gone. He looked at his hand in the dim light. The bite marks were there, but the swelling was not, it was not tender to touch. He wiggled his fingers. He looked at the girl. She was staring at the fire. He considered that he might be dreaming still and caught himself glancing around for Old Dave Wednesday. He looked up through the smoke at the dark sky. It was a clear night, deep, blue-black. He spotted a shooting star. He turned his head to see if the child had seen it also and she had.

She made a sign that Sam assumed meant star or shooting star. He repeated it back to her.

She nodded, smiled.

Sam felt good. He pulled away the flap of his ripped trouser leg and tried to observe that bite, but couldn't see it. He put his fingers to the site of the bite and it did not feel swollen. It was not tender either.

He stood and offered his hand to help Penny to her feet. Let's move on, he said and pointed his hand west. He thought to but did not kick out the fire. He stood in the middle of the smoke for a few seconds. He walked over and put the girl on the horse and they walked on. After about a quarter-mile, the headlights of a vehicle appeared, flashed, then steadied. Sam took the flashlight he had strapped to the saddle horn and waved it back and forth over his head.

The 4x4 stopped and three men got out. Sam couldn't make them out, but he recognized the sheriff's voice calling out to him.

When their faces were clear, Penny went running to one of the men. Sam knew it was her father. The third man was a county paramedic. Sam had seen him before, but didn't know his name.

How you doing? Dale asked.

Sam knew he looked confused, out of it, but that was, strangely, because he felt perfectly fine. I think I'm okay, he said.

Let me see the bites, the paramedic said.

Sam held out his hand. The symptoms went away, he said. Just like that. No chills, no swelling, nothing.

The medic shined his light on the wound. Well, there is a bite here, all right. But there's no swelling. I don't have to tell you that's a good thing. Must have been a dry bite.

Sam nodded. He didn't mention that it had been swollen. And on the back of my leg, here. He pulled away the pant leg.

The paramedic whistled. Yep, another one. I see you cut yourself. No swelling here either. Two dry bites. I'd play the lottery tonight, if I were you. You up-to-date with your tetanus shot?

Sam said he was.

The medic had Sam sit on the ground and took his blood pressure. He whistled again. One-twenty over eighty.

Dale looked at Sam's face. You all right?

Sam nodded. Apparently. He stood.

The girl's father came and hugged Sam. Thank you, he said. Thank you for finding my Penny.

You're welcome, Sam said, unsure. The fact that he felt perfectly well was unsettling and disorienting. He let out a long breath. He looked down at Penny, nodded, and signed, friend.

She signed back, but Sam didn't understand.

What did she say? Sam asked her father.

She said you will be fine now.

Sam looked at her eyes. She hugged his legs and he put his hand against her back. He dropped to a knee and hugged her back. He was so confused. He didn't know why he was not light-headed and nauseated and sweaty. Feeling healthy had never felt so strange. He looked at the girl's father.

She's special, the man said.

Yes, she is, Sam said.

The sheriff put his hand on Sam's shoulder.

Sam looked at the stars.

I know you're exhausted.

Sam nodded, but said nothing. On the contrary, he felt remarkably rested. Except for his profound confusion, he felt very well. You call Sophie?

I did. She's on her way.

The paramedic shook his head again. I ain't never seen two dry bites. The wounds don't look a bit angry.

Let's not look a gift horse in the mouth, the sheriff said. I reckon I'll ride the horse on back.

No, Dale, he's got a cracked hoof. I'll walk him back. You go back with the girl. The sheriff moved to protest. Really, Sam said. I need to be alone with my thoughts for a short while.

Okay, Doc, you got it.

I'll stay with you, the paramedic said.

Thanks, but I want you to ride back with them.

The young man looked at the sheriff and the sheriff nodded for him to get in the vehicle.

Penny left her father and stood again in front of Sam. She signed friend. The one word, as if she were speaking to a child. Then she signed what Sam understood to be thank you.

Thank you, he said. He signed her name.

The hike back to the staging area passed in what seemed normal time, not the protracted moment that Sam had imagined or maybe wished for, with no revelations and thankfully no replaying of the episode. He thought about a lot of things, his life, his practice, all the mundane thoughts that might have gone through his head during a drive home. The horse's limp was almost imperceptible, but it was there. He wended his way back through the same narrow wash he'd taken when he set out. When he emerged he saw Sophie leaning against a pickup talking to Eddie Yellow Calf. An electric lantern glowed weakly behind them on the hood. They were the only ones there and this relieved Sam. The horse huffed and drew attention. Sophie trotted to him. He hugged her and she then pushed herself back to look him over.

I'm all right, he said.

Dale told me that. He also told me a snake bit you.

Two snakes, Sam said. A little one and a big one. Seems snakes like me. But I don't think they were very good at being rattlers.

You're okay?

He nodded. The medic checked me out. Dry bites, we guess. Sam looked at her face. It was difficult to see her clearly in the shadows of the rocks. You're tired, he said. You should have driven out here.

Shut up.

Sophie clung to him as they walked toward Eddie. Zip ran around them, getting underfoot.

Eddie reached for the reins as they drew near. What did you do to my horse? He asked.

Flat tire, Sam said. Send me the bill. Split hoof. I'm not trying to make excuses, but it's been cracked for a while.

What do you know? You're just a vet. Eddie nodded. I glad you're all right.

Thanks, Eddie. Sam sat on the big black bumper of Eddie's truck, rubbed Zip's ears. Sophie stood beside him and rubbed his shoulders. Eddie removed the saddle and blanket and felt the horse's back. We'll he's cool.

He didn't carry me back.

Sam looked around. The moonlight showed what was left of the camp and staging area. There was the fire pit, the folding chair in which Sadie had sat, and a discarded pint milk carton. Sam walked over to the carton. He expected his knees and back to complain as he stooped to pick up the trash, but neither did.

You really get bit? Eddie asked.

Twice.

Eddie whistled. What happened?

I died.

Well, you look it.

Sam looked at Sophie. She nodded.

Et tu.

The spirits were with you, Eddie said. That's all I can say. The spirits were with you.

Sam tried not to roll his eyes. Spirits might not have been there, he thought, but Penny was there.

Eddied lowered the ramp of the horse trailer. The squeak of it bounced off the rocks. Pretty cool, he said. Getting to be the hero and all. You saved that little girl. Hero.

Sam smiled awkwardly, turned to Sophie. There was some saving going on, but not by me.

Well, if it weren't for you, she'd be out there freezing to death, Eddie said. He loaded the horse, pushed up the gate.

Maybe, Sam said. Tell me, what do you know about little Penny?

Don't know her. Never seen her. I know she's deaf. Heard she's a healer, got a gift. Hell everybody's kid's got a gift these days. My kid has the eating gift. He can eat groceries until he's tired. Yep, everybody's little muffin is special.

I reckon.

You're pretty good at that cowboy talk, ain't you.

I reckon.

Eddie fell in behind the wheel and closed his door. Don't you lovebirds stay out here too long. He drove away.

Sophie and Sam got into the car. Zip settled in on the back seat. She drove them home. It was cold, but Sam kept his window down.

Is this air bothering you? he asked.

No. Everything okay over there?

Apparently. But you're going to have stop asking me if I'm all right. I'm going to have to stop asking myself. Fact is, I can't believe I'm all right.

What happened out there?

Sam took his time and told her the whole story in as much detail as he could remember. He left out the part about Old Dave Wednesday. And then I walked the horse back and found you waiting there with Eddie.

Just another day at the office.

More or less.

What do you think?

What do I think about what?

You know, she said. Did that little girl heal your bites?

Sam looked out the window at the passing landscape. He said nothing.

Sam?

I should have played the lottery today, like the paramedic said.

The sky was so clear. The moon was so bright. Sam fell asleep, the glass of the window cold against his temple.

The sunlight glanced through the part in the curtains. Sam knew that he had overslept before he opened his eyes. He lay there and focused on the clock by his bedside. He was again bugged by the flaw that the hour hand was always a little ahead of the time and so he could never quickly read the time. It was nine-thirty. He hadn't slept past nine in ages, not even when he was sick with the flu. He could feel he was in the bed alone even before he heard the noises downstairs in the kitchen. He didn't remember getting into bed. He didn't remember taking off his clothes. The last thing he recalled was looking at the sky and feeling the cold air on his face. If he had dreamed during his long sleep, they were lost into wherever dreams get lost. He should have let Sophie hang a dream catcher over their bed way back when. Zip came and sat a few feet from him. He put out his hand and she walked over and rubbed her head under it. At least I'm in the right house, he said to her.

He sat up and put his feet on the floor, looked out the window, stretched. He felt awake, strong. He looked at the sites of his bites and saw the marks, but nothing bad. He showered, pulled on some jeans and a tee shirt and walked downstairs to the kitchen. Sophie was sitting at the table with her coffee.

I really slept, he said.

You didn't move all night.

I don't even think I dreamed.

Well, you had quite a day—night. How do you feel?

Great. What about you? You were up late, too.

I'm okay, she said. I kept waking up to make sure you were alive.

Was I?

Pretty much.

Alex Dimitrov
This Is Not a Personal Poem

This is not a personal poem.
I don't write about my life.
I don't have a life.
I don't have sex.
I have not experienced death.
Don't take this personally but
I don't have any feelings either.
The feelings I don't have don't run my life.
I have an imagination. I'm imagining it now.
This poem is concerned with language on a very plain level.
This poem stole that line from John Ashbery.
This poem wants you to like it,
please click "like."
This poem was written during a recession.
I'm so politically conscious
the word "politics" is in my poem.
This is not a New York poem.
There's not enough room for all the wars in this poem.
Gay marriage is now in this poem.
Have you liked this poem yet?
It was written in 2011 in New York and posted 11 minutes ago.
Would you sleep with the poet who wrote this poem?

Would you buy his book? Click here.
This poem loves language.
This poem has slept with other poems
written by poets who love language.
All poets love language.
Let's talk about language while people die.
This poem cares a lot but wants you
to think that it doesn't really care.
The speaker of this poem may have been
born in a former Communist country.
It may or may not matter.
I had an orgasm before writing this poem.
I have my sunglasses on while reading this poem.
Everyone is going to die
please don't take it personally.
The world. The world.
The world is blood-hot and personal.
I stole that line from Sylvia Plath.
Put your money on this poem.
I love the money shot.
This is not a personal poem.
This poem is only about Alex Dimitrov.

Self-Portrait Without the Self

On the edges of the body is where I stood,
trying to feel my way to the center.

For years, it was all I wanted.
Clawing at the small cells,

kicking in the bones to make room
for something more permanent.

And this morning, tired of my lips,
the way my hair will sometimes tilt

to one side, a lover of extremes,
every part of me, slanted

as if toward another body—
I no longer want the center:

this heart, or what's in it.
I want what isn't mine

and what will not last.
And yes, your heart will not last.

The Burning Place

These godless hours remain
the mind's faithful partner.
And from the only body I'll have,

I watch your motion, I watch you let me in.

Sontag recognized love is about submission.
Like giving yourself to be flayed and knowing
that any moment the other person can walk off

with your skin, she wrote.
If red is what I wear to dinner with you
to protect the skin I should give up.

If I say what you refuse to feel

and gladly take you to the burning place.
Where there is no you or I
and our veins, like graves, are opening

for what will open in us.
We start and finish one another with a kiss,
a look. We do it ruthlessly and all the time.

Michael Broek
Trans-Martini

69.
I
want to argue
because
my clock believes it is daylight savings time
and in fact my time
contains nothing that will be saved.

I
want to disavow
because
you have accused me of drinking too much
and I want to insist clear is blue
even though topsy is turvy and pour me another.

I
want to arm wrestle a French
theorist, kiss him on the nose tip
right before I slam his
arm into the counter
the one tattooed with the name of his last lover.

Eve, my sweet
mother of all the losses
you've laid at my feet. I deserve them.
My Adam, myself
is a man I'm just beginning to know
names wrongly.

It is all sound and strum and swaying hip
pressed onto hip, lap, breast, cradle and verve
slosh and bowl and drain and drip, not this and that
tyranny of the noun, rather pink and slow and hateful and
slick and vibrate and penultimate, precise, perambulations
around the Garden,
tea set in the basket, bottle of Pinot buried
under the rise, where all the slovenly wilderness
rises up to greet the mother and father of love.

Make love to me! You great
un-collected gathering storm. You lightning storm.
You port. You river. You arm of fingers, neck, and bones.

Sinning

There is no soup today.
Only bread. Without crust.
The impossible soft middle. The baker's hand
forming a long rising loaf, like a body,
and the skin, delicious and thin.
So much Adam's apple. Biting there.
We could live on such violations for centuries.
What did it mean? To snip the tenuous
threads of decorum, doing what we are told.
For how long?
Really? One day
there is no soup. The next,
no bread—
your slim neck in my hands,
the rising, the falling,
the split second between. That's the revolution.

Ben Stroud
Amy

I had been in Wiesbaden for two weeks. This was October 2009. The German semester, and with it my job, hadn't yet started, and after a first week surrendered to various bureaucracies, I was spending a chain of sunny days exploring. On the third such day, after taking the little yellow funicular up the Neroberg and hiking down, I was walking in the pedestrian-zoned city center and had paused to look through the window of the gummy candy store. Thoughts of a present shipped home to my nephews had taken breath then perished (the postage, the hassle) when someone behind me said "Holy shit" and grabbed me by the arm.

The words with their three flat American syllables leaped at me from the constant guttural hum and I turned to find a short, nicely thick-bodied woman with round, light-green eyes and hair of rusted blond that fell in limp strands just past her shoulders. I knew her, but my memory fumbled until immediately I had a flash of her at fifteen: studded leather choker around her neck, bottle of cherry soda constantly stowed in her backpack, Mod-Podged collages of ads from *Spin* magazine covering her folders. Amy Heathcock. She'd been two years behind me in high school, and we'd been members of separate outcast cliques that sometimes joined and that shared the hallway outside the band hall for hanging out in the mornings before class. Once we'd gone on a date, and later, when I was home from college, I ran into her at the Corny Dog in the Longview Mall, where she dipped hot dogs in batter. But by the time she clutched my arm in Langgasse I'd forgotten she existed.

"What are you doing here?" she said. She smiled and freed her other hand from a stroller to pull me into a hug.

"I'm teaching," I said. I neglected to mention I was also fleeing a failing marriage, which was arguably the truer answer. "What about you?"

"I'm staying with a friend," she said. The friend's husband was army, she explained, stationed at the airfield outside of town, and they lived in one of the blocks of married housing on the other side of the train station. I nodded. The day before, I'd taken a bus in that direction and seen a Popeye's and a Taco Bell locked behind a tall, guarded fence. "This is my Macy," Amy added, looking down at the two-year-old who lay in the stroller's seat, passed out. "She likes it when I push her through here. Sometimes it's all I can do to get her to sleep." Amy looked up again. In that moment she seemed barely changed in the decade-plus from the girl I remembered. The same freckled nose with its mousy tip, the same sly light in her eyes, the same pull of tee shirt fabric across the same soft pouch of belly. She said we should hang out and I agreed.

We went to the Café Maldaner, just around the corner, where we picked slices of cake from a glass case and sat in the high-ceilinged, wood-paneled tearoom. I'd wanted to go inside the Maldaner since I first saw it. According to the gold lettering on the window it dated to 1859, and I imagined Dostoevsky, who'd lived here in the 1860s, drinking coffee inside as he fretted about the previous evening's losses at the gaming tables and brooded over the hazy, just-forming figures that would, in short time, solidify into Raskolnikov and Sonia, Porfiry Petrovitch and Razumikhin.

As we sat, Amy tended to her daughter. She had woken and, after staring silently at me for three minutes ("Macy, this is one of Mommy's friends," Amy had said), she started throwing her toys at a mink-coated frau whose spun sugar sphere of white hair evidently made for an irresistible target. The toys kept landing short, and I would pick them up and give them to Amy, who would give them back to the crying Macy, who would throw them again. I wondered if this was all that would happen and if it was for the best. But after Macy's fit, as Amy asked me about high school—who I still saw, if I remembered this or that drama—she took my hand, and once we finished our cake I walked her to my apartment. There we parked Macy in front of the TV, which I turned to Kika, the children's channel, and we went into the bedroom. As we stood together, Amy's back pressed against me, I lifted her skirt and bit her neck. She squealed—I remembered that squeal, heard sometimes outside the band hall whenever another sex-deprived, aching boy poked or tickled her generous flesh. Then she told me to hurry. We only had until the cartoon ended.

*

After we finished she wheeled Macy out of my apartment, and I sat down to work on my syllabi. I'd given Amy my phone number and my email address, but as I looked at my laptop's screen I hoped that was it, that she would step back into her life and I into mine. The last thing I wanted was a new entanglement.

So when she called me a few days later, asking if I'd like to meet her, I was worried.

"Just for an hour," she said.

"My wife," I said.

"You said you haven't talked to her in a month."

"Macy."

"I'll leave her with Beth."

She waited while I said nothing. I found myself thinking of the large, milk-white breasts that I'd admired at sixteen and that, as we'd stood in my bedroom, had remained bound behind her bra, unexplored.

"I'm not sure," I said.

"Think of it this way. We're friends. What's wrong with being friends?"

But we'd never been friends. She was just a girl I'd happened to know years ago. Still, it was enough. Two hours later I was waiting for her outside the Karstadt, one of the massive, glass-walled shopping centers downtown. She showed wearing jeans and hoop earrings, and I felt twelve years younger, the entirety of my life spread before me, unmade.

My wife sat enshrined chief among the litter of disappointments and mistakes I'd come to Germany to escape. I met her in my third year at Michigan, when she was a first-year fresh from a small liberal arts college in Maine. Clara came from an old-money family of Chicago lawyers, bred for summers at Saugatuck and seats on museum boards, and attended our graduate seminars in peasant dresses no peasant could afford and high leather boots that pressed smoothly against her calves. At parties she would stand in the corner telling practiced stories to a small, rapt circle of fellow students clutching bottles of Oberon or Winter White. About the night the president (before he was president) came for cocktails: "He had really hairy ears. You'd think someone would tell him." About the year after her parents' divorce: "I met my dad each week at this Chinese place. I always ordered the Happy Family." A pause, then a half-smile. "He never got the joke."

That I made her love me, that I somehow entered her existence and found a place in it—the comfiest chair in the living room of her soul—I still count as the greatest accomplishment of my reinvention. I had been a sweaty, acned nobody from a small town in East Texas that most people had never heard of, then a scholarship student at the state university with no claim on anything higher than the dreary futures (pharmaceutical sales, a chain store's management track) touted at the job fairs held each year in our basketball arena. But a marathon semester spent polishing an application essay ended with me in a grad program where my peers were people with the kinds of East Coast, private school educations I had long envied. By the time I met Clara I had transformed myself, through the alchemy of a research assistantship with a famous theorist and a paper on Spinoza and Coleridge given at a major conference, into a promising scholar, a rising star of the department. I was climbing, never so sure of what I was climbing toward until I saw Clara standing in her circle—her hair loose over her temples, her upper lip pooched by the slightest of overbites—exuding class privilege like a musk.

She showed wearing jeans and hoop earrings, and I felt twelve years younger, the entirety of my life spread before me, unmade.

We married a year later. The ceremony was small, in the chapel of a large downtown Chicago church, St. James Episcopal. The other graduate students dubbed us the power couple and we took an apartment in a house in the Old West Side with a porch we'd sit on when it was warm, drinking gin and tonics, and two spare rooms we used as offices. Clara dressed me in thrift store blazers, idly ran her fingers through my thinning hair while she read. In the summer we spent long weeks at her family's place on Lake Michigan, swimming and working through stacks of books. Our happiness seemed unquestionable. But the following spring, after a semester spent trying to break ground on my dissertation ("Representations of Eastern Europeans in the Nineteenth-Century Novel," chosen after a misleadingly exuberant seminar) I had a crisis. I saw all my future years spent waking to wrestle with murky thoughts, to put cold words on cold pages no one would ever read. It was a rather mundane crisis, my adviser told me, but I didn't get over it. Meanwhile, Clara had turned into a plodding worker, in her office every morning, and only now that we were married did I discover that what I'd thought was a quiet, aristocratic disdain was instead pure shyness, that her affected coolness shrouded a sentimental heart. I had expected the air in this new world to which I'd laid claim to be different, to ease me past imperfection and strife in a narcotic mist. But sealed together in that house, Clara and I began to fight. Usually I was the provoker, coming to Clara with some correction I though she could make to her habits or person (the dissertation abandoned, I had little else to brood about). At first, whenever I caught the sound of her crying behind her office door, I'd go to her, apologize, but eventually I chose to ignore her muffled sobs and instead waited for her to come out to dinner, amnesic smile pinned to her face. When, at the end of summer, I told her about the job in Germany, a one-year exchange appointment at the university in Mainz that I'd begged from the grad director, she said she didn't want me to go, but within a day she'd packed my things in a box.

Amy and I began meeting on Mondays and Fridays. I taught the other days of the week, and the weekends, I told her, I needed for grading, though in fact I simply wanted to keep them to myself. Sometimes we took trips: In Bad Homburg we strolled through the Kurpark with its Thai temples and miniature Russian church, then toured the Kaiser's summer palace where the guide showed us first the Kaiser's telephone cabinet, with its private line to Berlin, then the Kaiser's flush toilet, with its view over the palace roof. In Höchst we wandered into the toll castle's moat, a green, ivy-strewn park abandoned that day under a gray sky, and in Rüdesheim we sat on a rock in a muddy, bare vineyard, getting drunk on grape brandy while we watched the Rhine flow by, its long, thin cargo barges easing their way to Rotterdam. On our trips I found it difficult to contain myself. In the vineyard I brought her head to my lap and unzipped my jeans as hikers passed a hundred feet above us, and in the Höchst moat I leaned her into a corner and slipped my fingers inside her waistband before a man overhead whistled, his head poking out from the castle's high tower, which cost a euro to climb.

The days we didn't take trips we spent in my apartment, and the days we did take trips we always ended there. As soon as we closed the door we'd shed our clothes and scurry to bed, me getting up and dressing only to fetch our dinner from the dimly lit takeaway—Indian food, pizza, schnitzels—four doors down. We never talked of our lives beyond the age of nineteen, only of prom, football games, and the bored, unending nights spent driving the Longview loop. One afternoon Amy went through the catalog of girls we'd known, asking which ones I'd had crushes on, and giggled any time I said yes and for at least two declared, "Skank!" Another time I brought up our date.

She blushed. "I was wondering when you'd ask about that."

"So you do remember?"

She looked at me. "What about you? What do you remember?"

"You barely spoke to me. I took you to the Jalapeño Tree and we ate fajitas, then I asked you what you wanted to do and somehow we ended up at a soccer game. We sat in my car and all I wanted to do the whole time was feel you up, but I could tell you just wanted to go home."

"I was horrible!" she said. "I was really into you when you asked me out but by the end of the week I wasn't. I was like that all sophomore year." Then she kicked back the sheets and sat atop me, leaning down so that her breasts pressed against my chest. "Have I made up for it now?"

She had.

Since arriving in Wiesbaden, I'd been trying, off and on, to find out where Dostoevsky had lived during his time in the city. I'd had no luck (even Google had turned up nothing) until early in November, when I spent an afternoon hiking on the Neroberg. At the Russian cemetery I happened upon a faded display, in Russian and German, recording the history of Russian notables in the area, and next to Dostoevsky's name I saw *Hotel Viktoria*.

I was going to wait until Saturday to look for the hotel, but Amy said she wanted to come with me. As we were walking together down Wilhelmstrasse, the street where most of the old spa hotels had stood, she asked me what I wanted to find. The truth was I hadn't read Dostoevsky since college. But he'd lived in Wiesbaden, and now I did: there was hope in the parallel, depth I could glom. If nothing else, the search for his hotel would be a good detail to drop over drinks whenever I returned home. Before I could make up some different, better answer, though, Amy took my hand in hers and swung it a little and said, "If you were a writer, what would you write about me?"

I thought for a moment. We passed the Meissen shop, its porcelain goat staring mutely through the window, and then I said, "That you had nice thighs and you helped me through a bad time."

The question had been asked in a jokey tone, and I had answered in a jokey tone, but at my reply she grew quiet.

After we walked another block she slipped her hand from mine.

"I'm sorry," I said. "I'm not sure what you wanted me to say."

"Nothing," she said. "I was just being stupid." When I glanced at her she smiled. I was practiced at detecting false smiles, but I was practiced at ignoring them, too.

I'd asked about the old Hotel Viktoria in the tourist office, and the woman behind the counter had first consulted a book and then made a phone call before telling me that it stood on the northeast corner of Wilhelmstrasse and Rheinstrasse. We arrived there now and I stopped and looked up. The Viktoria was dressed in red stone and had curving, wrought iron balconies. It wasn't a hotel anymore but offices, its bottom floors given over to an interior design firm and a shop selling ballet clothes. In the summer of 1865 Dostoevsky had holed up here and feverishly churned out his first draft of *Crime and Punishment.* Judging by the names on the plate next to the main door, his room belonged now to either a notary or a foot doctor. I'd expected

I was climbing, never so sure of what I was climbing toward until I saw Clara standing in her circle—her hair loose over her temples, her upper lip pooched by slightest overbite—exuding class privilege like musk.

to feel something, for inspiration to zap out from the stones and grip me, but it was just a building.

Later, as we lay in bed, bellies full of chicken korma from down the street, Amy's head resting on my chest, she said, "I like you." Since our conversation on Wilhelmstrasse, things had been unsettled between us. "I like being with you, OK?"

"OK," I said. "I like being with you, too."

A few days later, Clara called. It was a Thursday and I'd spent the day teaching and had had to keep reminding myself that it was actually Thanksgiving. Clara and I hadn't talked in two months, and after she wished me a happy Thanksgiving we didn't say much else until she asked, "Are you flying home for Christmas?"

"I'm not sure," I said.

"Do you want to fly back?"

I didn't say anything.

"I need to know what to tell my parents."

"I know," I said.

"Well, what should I tell them?"

There was the slightest quaver in her voice. I couldn't hear the murmur of family behind her. She must have been up in her room, sitting on her bed, the door shut. In my mind I saw her there, the lights turned off and light coming in from the street, her face pointed toward the stable of horse figurines from her girlhood. Through the deadness of my heart I felt a throb.

"Well?" she said again.

I told her, "I'm not sure," and she hung up.

The phone call was still troubling me when, a day later, Amy and I were sitting in bed. It was rainy and cold and we'd stayed in. Pulling closer to me, Amy told me that she and Macy were going to Rothenburg with Beth and her husband next week and she wanted me to come with them.

"Seriously?" I said.

"It'll be fun."

I tried to picture the five of us on a jaunt together. I couldn't.

"No, I don't think so," I said, and added something about grading.

She put a leg on top of mine, rested her chin on my chest, and looked at me. She was smiling, but I didn't know how long I had.

"Fine," I said. "OK. Yes."

The following Friday, the day set for the trip, a red, beat-up Opel honked for me at nine. After I came out Amy introduced me to Beth and her husband as her friend, and I was given the passenger seat. Amy and Beth sat together in the back, Macy buckled into her car seat directly behind me. When we drove off I glanced at the husband, Wesley. We'd been at war for eight years and I hadn't yet talked to a soldier. His face was red and pitted and his upper lip bore a sparse brown mustache. I didn't know what to say to him.

As he guided us out of town he didn't speak, but once we were on the highway he started talking. He drifted from the trips he and Beth took to Cologne and Neuschwanstein to karaoke at the Irish pub to run-ins between his fellow soldiers and the *polizei*—one soldier caught flying up the autobahn, drunk, throwing beer bottles at the cars coming the other direction, another found passed out in his car, four in the morning, beneath a traffic light deep in the Wiesbaden suburbs. "Don't fuck with the *polizei*," he warned me. "They'll fine your ass." I waited for an opportune moment to mention my father's combat in Vietnam. Those few times I felt guilt over not going to war in this our decade of troubles, he was my excuse. He did that, so I didn't have to, was my thinking—he'd actually said that to me once. But Wesley didn't bring up Iraq or Afghanistan, though Amy told me he'd been to both, and at the end of each of his stories I simply smiled and laughed politely.

We arrived at Rothenburg and the place was already filled with tourists, half of them American: I spotted their SUVs in the parking lot, imported Explorers and Denalis with Frankfurt or Munich plates, the owners army officers or expat bankers. After we found our own spot, we walked in through a gate in the town wall; I pushed Macy's empty stroller while Amy held her. At the *platz* a brass band played in the Christmas market and crowds swelled like tides beneath the high old buildings. We bought sausages and *glühwein* from a booth, then started the cycle through the tidy medieval streets. A couple times Amy took pictures of me and Macy in front of a fountain or one of the leaning, timbered houses. I wasn't sure what to do with her—I'd only seen Macy a couple times since that day in Langgasse—and I held her awkwardly against my chest or rested my palm on her head as she squirmed next to my leg. By the third picture I began to get nervous. I said something to Amy about it and she gave me a blank look and said, "I just want some pictures." I let it go.

"Jason would have loved this," Wesley said, stopped in front of a shop selling souvenir knives. Jason was Amy's ex-husband, from whom, she'd told me, she'd gotten divorced a year ago. That's how Amy and Beth had met; army wives at Fort Bragg. But Wesley's eyes were red. I looked to Amy and she was teary, too, and at that I felt the bottom of my stomach sink open. Amy caught me looking and said, "Please. We'll talk tonight." I stayed quiet. We left soon after.

When the red Opel pulled up to my apartment, Amy got out. She kissed the still-sleeping Macy on the forehead, then asked Beth, "You're sure you don't mind?" and Beth waved her toward me.

Once inside she told me what I'd already figured out, that she'd lied about the divorce and Jason was dead. He'd been killed a year ago in Afghanistan. I started to say something, though I had no idea what, and she stopped me before I could.

"I needed to talk to you about all this tonight anyway. You get to stay ninety days without a visa."

"OK," I said.

"My ninety days are about to run out."

I was a little stunned. "Really?" I said.

"I've got ten days—I have to leave a week from Monday. But if we got a civil union . . ." She broke off, glanced away.

"I'm married," I said.

"You could divorce."

"That would take time."

"Only thirty days in Michigan. I looked it up. I could go home, then come back once you were divorced."

I felt the blood drain from my body, the newly risen ghost of her husband sitting in the corner of the room. "My visa's only good until August," I said, to say something. But she knew I'd been offered an extra year. Despite myself, I'd kept the university here happy. Unlike my predecessors, I had resisted throwing stacks of student essays in the toilet or claiming that people in the department were passing secret messages in their lectures.

In my mind I saw her there, the lights turned off and light coming in from the street, her face pointed toward the stable of horse figurines from her girlhood. Through the deadness of my heart I felt a throb.

"It's not just that," she said. "I like you. I've been thinking about us, together."

She seemed her prettiest then, looking up at me. She shook with a slight tremor—she was fighting hard. And the truth was, I liked her too. But as I stood over her, the twelve years that usually disappeared when we were together returned. All I could see was her watching her old reality TV shows dubbed in German, Macy throwing a fit, and me, who liked a silent apartment filled with nothing but the noise that drifted from the street, trying to read behind a shut door.

I told her she was being ridiculous, this wasn't what I'd wanted, and how could I trust her after today. For a moment her face remained still, but then she bolted up, hand jerked over her eyes to keep me from seeing them, and rushed out. I stood there and watched her go.

Nearly a month later, the week after Christmas, I flew to London, summoned by Clara. Her sister lived in the Surrey suburbs, and Clara had flown over to visit.

She asked me to come for a day, and there wasn't a way for me to say no. I took a late flight and spent the night in a bland business-traveler's hotel near Heathrow. Clara's sister's husband, still technically my brother-in-law, booked for me with his points.

In the morning I took a cab to Windsor Great Park, where I was to meet Clara beside Virginia Water. The cab driver dropped me off in a parking lot, and beyond the lot spread the park, or one corner of it. People were out, walking dogs they'd dressed in raincoats and plaid, quilted capes. The trees were lifeless, their bare limbs seemingly all that kept the gray, pressing clouds from tumbling to earth.

Clara was up ahead, her back to me as she watched the swans floating in the icy water of the lake. I called to her, and she turned. There was her auburn hair, spilling out of her parka's hood, there was her dainty pointed nose, red at the tip with cold. Seeing her, I felt the last months erased, as if I'd just come up from a dream.

"Do you want anything?" I asked, nodding at the concession cart a hundred yards away.

"Tea," she said.

I'd been nervous ever since Clara called to ask me over, and as I waited for the tea and my hot chocolate I studied the cart's case of British snacks and tried to think through what I might do next. I had a suspicion of what was happening, but still my mind refused to work.

After I gave Clara her tea we took the path that went to the right, up the eastern branch of the lake. For a while we said nothing and watched the trotting dogs. Then, as I was testing my hot chocolate—still scalding—Clara said, "Do you plan to move back in with me next summer?"

The question startled me, though that had been the plan once, the idea that Germany would be a cure.

"I don't know," I said. "I've been trying not to think about it."

There was a pause. Then, with a changed, efficient tone I'd never heard from her before, she said, "Good. That's all I needed to hear."

I stopped, but she kept walking. I jogged to catch up with her. "What do you mean?"

"I'm going to file for divorce."

As we walked she kept a few inches between us. I sipped my hot chocolate. It was cooler now.

"Don't worry," she said. "I'll let you know what you need to do."

In that moment I decided the last thing I wanted was to cause her more pain, so I told her I'd do whatever she asked.

We passed through a part of the path lined on both sides with chain link fence. Behind the fence workmen had left tools and some kind of tractor.

"What have you been up to, anyway?" she said.

"Fucking a war widow," I answered. I tried to smile, like it was some kind of joke, and only when I kept walking did I notice that this time she'd stopped. I turned and saw she'd started to cry. I went to her, but she batted me away. Dog walkers passed us, shifting their eyes.

"Really?" she said. "That's what you're going to say?"

I tried to put my arm around her, but she backed away. "You don't deserve anything," she said, and the words cut like broken glass.

I flew back to Frankfurt. On the plane I tried an exercise whereby I emptied my mind bit by bit. It didn't work.

From the airport I took the S-Bahn to Wiesbaden, and as we came to a river, the Main, I looked up, as I always do for rivers. I'd taken an early flight. The Main was still and narrow, and as we turned to cross it the morning sun shot through the windows and the river glistened. Across from me two plump girls with spiked, raven hair giggled over their cell phones, indifferent, their thick thighs stretching the weave of their matching leopard-print tights, their stout, pimpled faces held close together. In the aisle a Turk or a Romany, accordion folded shut and slung over his shoulder, shook his knitted change purse. I closed my eyes and listened as the train clacked over the bridge. I felt Clara's words, Amy's silence, wounds beneath my skin. But as the rare winter sun shone on my face I said to myself: *I am blameless.* I said: *I owe no one.* I said: *Surely something better has been promised me.*

Bruce Bond
The Smokers

It goes against our deepest instincts,
the Buddha who, eyes closed, breathes the tar
of another's suffering, then releases

the body's reservoir of light, taking
on a pain that is, by nature, a thing
we cannot take, we cannot take away.

So why bother after all. Why drink
imaginary poison, as if the motions
of life would dust the jewel in our chest.

Perhaps we, who know so little sleep,
glide into a harbor made of fog
and lower anchor there. Take my friend

who grew so weary of the obvious,
who lit one Camel with the last, and yes,
he quit, as if it mattered, as if the final

ditch could save him. His wife quit as well,
late, then took it up again in mourning.
It kept her company, like the scent

that hung among the shirts in her closet.
With every match she cradled, she passed
a torch from one craving to another,

as she did when they first talked, alone,
high on the steps of a small museum.
Just the specks of them and the night sky,

how it glimmered as their embers breathed,
each a momentary pulse, responding,
an ache to feed the sweetness of the smoke.

Follow

My mother's journey was a nail
that drove always in one direction,

deeper into the hard part, until the day
it stopped, complete, fully seated in the darkness.

Pain is pain, I do not doubt that,
but more than this, she argued bitterly with time

to turn back, as if every throb
was the bell of some cathedral, some message

sent out to a sky that never responded.
One direction, like the face we live in,

the one we push ahead to shield us from the blows.
All her life she prepared for a season she knew

so little about, where she would wander
late and listen to the clocks, where they chipped the huge

rock of silence. Whatever it was the chimes said,
it was obsolete the moment that they said it.

A body moves, and we follow. Like it or not,
she follows me still. This is what it means to obey.

Jynne Dilling Martin
Autopsies Were Made with the Following Results

I draw uncounted fugues from pianos but no consolation,
and recall the ogre who mistook hot coals for roasted nuts,

and dream of riding atop my sadness like it is a horse.
My horse may be black yet in darkness is easily mounted,

and the coals may have long collapsed into ash, but the burn
on the tongue remains. The children dance, the children sing:

touch teeth, touch leather, can't have back for ever and ever.
Just as a spun knife on a table will tell the future,

the thickness of anyone's ice will predict the past.
"You owe me an explanation!" I shout at the vanishing man,

and though I can disturb the quiet of the jungle with my cries,
I cannot force a fly to rip off its wings. I would like to strip you

naked and suspend you in a net, exposed to insect stings,
I would like to suck in your last exhale as you expire,

I wish we could begin again. Touch white, swap back if I like.
Just as a man of faith can carry off the ocean in a simple shell,

the fatalist who opens the piano lid must play on.
The oyster will not be sated until filled with pearl.

Alone We Were Though Never Left Alone

I can no longer trust other people. The cat grows gradually larger
as he steals along the trail. It sounds like a riddle but I will explain:

after a flood the quicksand remains, the river derailed quietly chews
at the floors of cemented basements. My own abscesses deepen every day.

As I sleep, your ghost slides in and out through my slackened mouth
and turns me into an animal waiting to die, hairless, dry-mouthed,

we forget our youthful fucking, our softness, how in ancient times we had tails.
We learn of our crimes from our dreams: large skins in barrels of brine

shaved off each other's bodies, we did this to one another, this ugly hunger,
grinded our knives as grain by grain the ocean swallowed the beach.

The earth is falling in a pin-straight line: it is space that curves around us,
we are doomed to orbit back into the maw of our mistakes,

discover the same hairs on our sheets, false hairs of various colors,
you promised it would be the last time that this happened.

I dreamt I swallowed the hairs of every betrayal. But her hair grew back.
It is the same cat, and he smiles, and will not stop walking toward me.

Christine Sneed
The New, All-True CV

24 April 2010

Dr. Sandra Matheson, Ph.D.
Executive Vice President of Human Resources
Elite Industries
4200 N. Prairie Blvd.
Omaha, NE 68182

Dear Dr. Matheson:

I am writing today to apply for the position of Chief Recruiter, Manufacturing
Division at Elite Industries, which I know from my research is the number-one
luxury tee shirt manufacturer in the Midwest, possibly in the United States, if not in
all of North America. Your tee shirts are the most stylish articles of clothing in my
closet, and I have been wearing your products for many years. My first Elite shirt
was long-sleeved and purple, and I purchased it at a Prince concert with a month's
worth of babysitting money when I was thirteen. I attended this concert with my
friend Elizabeth Perle who no longer speaks to me, but I'll save that story for later
on in my application. The Prince tee shirt, which is more than twenty-five years old
now, is still in excellent condition. On the front is a picture of the diminutive rock

star sitting on a motorcycle (the same image is on his *Purple Rain* album cover, one you might also be familiar with), and the dates and cities of his tour are printed on the back. The fabric and stitching have held up very well through countless washings, even if the silk screening hasn't fared as well. If you'd like, I can bring this shirt with me if you call me in for an interview (which of course I hope you will).

After thinking for a long time about the stressful process of applying and interviewing for jobs, and all that these processes entail, I have come to some conclusions about the methods employed by many HR departments in their day-to-day business of finding the best possible candidates for their companies' available positions. As the attached curriculum vitae details, I have a degree in both finance and management organizational behavior from The Ohio State University (the "the" with its capital T, for some reason, is very important to OSU functionaries, though I'm still not sure that I understand why), and I have some unorthodox (but potentially revolutionary) ideas about how to make more lasting hires for every position in any company. Like you, however, I am most interested in helping to ensure the ongoing success of the hiring process at Elite Industries. Vetting potential employees is a fraught undertaking, of course, and during the interview period, a recruiter can never be sure if a candidate is what he or she appears to be, either on paper or in person.

Although I realize that my CV should only stress the positive, my scholastic and professional accomplishments in particular, this document's viability is doomed from the outset because it omits some of the most remarkable formative events of my life, whether they are personal successes or humiliating but character-building failures. With this in mind, the attached document is my attempt to offer you a more detailed and genuine picture of who I am. Most of the following information would ordinarily never be a feature of any job application, but because I had a near-death experience not long ago (which is detailed on the attached, ref. Disasters, Averted or Otherwise), the same experience that eventually led me to come up with my innovative recruiting strategies, I have decided to dispense with the usual self-promoting subterfuge. As long as this impulse endures, I intend to embrace it, and I hope that you will be impressed and engaged by what you learn from my CV. (It should be noted that coworkers usually learn what a new hire's shortcomings are not long after he or she first sets foot in his/her new workplace.

Here I am bypassing this honeymoon period and will help to ensure that future Elite Industries candidates do the same if I am offered this position.)

Please feel free to contact me at your earliest convenience at either (213) 424-6158 or FanofElite@goodjob.com. I do hope to hear from you soon.

Sincerely yours,
Camille Roberts

ENCL: experimental CV
        sample interview questions

(Prototype: The New, All-True CV)

Camille Roberts
1624 N. Madison Dr.
Winfield, NE 68140
FanofElite@goodjob.com
cell: (213) 464-2535

OBJECTIVE: To acquire a prestigious and lucrative position in Elite's Human Resources department that will allow me to revolutionize hiring practices for current and future generations of workers. Also, to find love and marry above my current economic and social class. Husband-to-be will ideally have good teeth; a taut and well-muscled mid-section; no kids from previous wives or girlfriends; no credit card or gambling debts or outstanding student loans; no history of consorting with prostitutes; no substance abuse problems, including but not limited to cigarettes, alcohol, fatty foods, intravenous drugs and prescription pills; he will not have any visible disabilities such as a limp or psoriasis, will own his own home and will not spend whole weekends staring at the TV, cursing and cajoling various millionaire athletes as if he were their bipolar father.

FORMATIVE YEARS/EDUCATION:

Elementary & Junior High School
Northborough Elementary and Junior High Schools, Northborough, MA
    - *1978–79* - I don't think I was any more of a misfit than most, but I did have the unfortunate tendency of breaking out in facial hives whenever a teacher asked

me a question, and although I usually knew the answer, I hated to have everyone's demonic eyes staring at me, and soon they started to expect me to get hives and I always did, on some level not wanting to disappoint them, I guess, and also, I was so young and nervous by temperament, and had to eat ham-salad sandwiches for lunch more often than not, their smell aggressively permeating the orange-walled room where we all kept our sack lunches and coats and hats. On top of this, I had a well-meaning, secretary-pool mother who dressed me too primly in plaid skirts and buckle shoes and pigtails with ribbons. What young girl isn't painfully anxious about everything having to do with school and with boys who stepped on shy girl-classmates' toes to get their attention and called them Pimplehead and Piss-Pants for reasons that will not be explained here?

- *1979–80* - All families have similarities and differences, the voice on the filmstrip said, just as all girls and boys have similarities and differences. Something else I learned that year: it is never a good idea to walk into your parents' bedroom without knocking first, especially if you've had to skip your after-school Young Bible Scholars class because of an upset stomach, and therefore you arrive home early to discover what some of the main differences between boys and girls are. It is even more alarming if you walk in on your parents and one of them isn't actually your parent but the parent of a classmate who is known for stealing small, valuable objects from neighbors' houses, which, as an adult, you will later understand to be an act meant to punish his own parents rather than the people he stole from.

- *1982–83* - If you were female and grew to be five feet, seven inches tall by sixth grade and had largish front teeth that made you look, in some people's opinion, like a fur-bearing, rapidly reproducing creature, and you needed a bra as big as a few of your classmates' mothers' bras, bigger in a few cases, you learned early on that life isn't fair, that life is actually a cosmic joke played out over and over on the young who are sometimes desperate enough to consider suicide by mixing bleach and chocolate milk but (luckily) never find the guts to drink this lethal, disgusting beverage.

High School
Somerville High School, Somerville, MA
- *August 1986* - Shelly Zenk's party between freshman and sophomore years is a classic example of an event that is supposed to be lost in the sands of time but

fiercely refuses to be covered for any extended period. At Shelly's house, I suffered the indignity of getting my monthly visitor while wearing a white skirt and having to call my parents to pick me up early, along with a second, worse indignity of first having allowed myself to be felt up by a buffoon named Steve Lish who was known for eating oranges with the peels still on them, who often forgot to wear deodorant, and who, at a talent show in the eighth grade, burped the chorus to "Jessie's Girl" to great acclaim and eventual detention.

- *April 1987* - While babysitting for the Monroes who lived on Paradise Lane in a split-level with a stained glass window embedded in their front door that looked as if it had been stolen from a church, I went for a walk with the boy and girl I was in charge of for the night while the Monroes ate dinner at a fancy Indian restaurant near Harvard Square to celebrate their twelfth wedding anniversary. The boy and girl, Kyle and Alyssa, were riding in a wagon that I was pulling behind me, and they soon began giggling like asylum inmates. When I looked back to see why they were laughing, Kyle made an obscene hand gesture. In my embarrassed surprise, I accidentally overturned the wagon, both kids falling out, Kyle bumping his head on the sidewalk, and unfortunately, never being quite the same again. His parents didn't sue my parents because we weren't yet as litigious a society as we are today and Kyle's grades didn't get any worse; somehow they actually got better, but he acquired the habit of shouting at inappropriate times, often racial epithets or curse words that caused his parents to turn red and rush him out of movie theaters or away from the Fourth of July parade, and apparently, his sister to avoid him more and more as they grew older.

- *October 1988* - There was morning-after remorse but no unplanned pregnancy. There was a minor flare-up of something that required antibiotics and a humiliating conversation, conducted over the phone, with the boy in question who, to my amazement, did not go out and tell forty of his closest friends, but this might have been due in part to the motorcycle accident he had later that day, one where he broke his collarbone and the femur of his left leg. While he was in the hospital being plastered over, his parents found out what else was wrong with him and, too cowardly to admit to his own faults, he blamed the bacteria and burning sensation on me. His stepmother soon called my parents and demanded that they stop letting their whorish daughter out of the house. Shelly Zenk was once again implicated: it was through her that I met this diseased coward who, along with a motorcycle, had three pairs of football cleats, two pairs of soccer shoes, a father with three DUIs and a mother with another husband, another two sons, all living in another state in a far coastal city.

- *March 1989* - I let a different boy in the afternoon senior English class plagiarize my Hamlet paper, which turned out to be a very bad idea because Mr. Weir and Mrs. Pottsfield didn't believe that either of us had written it. Mr. Weir thought that Alex Crouse and I had gone in together and paid a smart kid from a nearby university to write it for us, because even though I earned good grades every quarter, I wasn't supposed to know who Laurence Olivier was, let alone enough about theater performance to comment on his interpretation of Hamlet, because what high school kid knew anything about the English stage, let alone Sir Laurence Olivier? What Mr. Weir and Mrs. Pottsfield didn't believe was that my parents had made me watch Olivier's *Hamlet* on PBS, and I had taken notes on the way he portrayed Hamlet's mental state—was the Danish prince as crazy and hysterical as Ophelia? I thought he was, but to make such an argument at age seventeen is to risk teacherly censure, especially when just a year earlier Mr. Weir had caught me taking a roll of toilet paper out of the girls' bathroom because I had a bad cold. But he thought that I planned to t.p. the trees outside the school, which had been happening a lot that fall term.

College

The Ohio State University, Columbus, OH, Bachelor of Science Degree, May 1993
Major - Business: Concentrations in Finance and Management Organizational Behavior (*I have no clear idea why I ended up majoring in these two disciplines. My temperament was probably better suited to a foreign language or an English literature degree, but from eighteen to twenty-one, it is very hard to know what you're truly interested in, aside from looking pretty, avoiding public disgrace, having sexual relations with people who might or might not hurt you [badly], and making friends with people who might or might not hurt you [badly] either.*)

- *Fall and spring semester, Freshman year, 1989–90* - Freud, Jung, and Poe: The id, the ego, the superego, the anima, the doppelganger, the telltale heart. These were costumes some of us learned to dress up in at will. In tandem, we were trying on promiscuity, duplicity, scorn, madness (real or imagined), genius (real or imagined), self-destruction, alcoholism, Catholicism, individuality, Judaism, classism, racism. In many cases, during high school, we had already developed an early mastery of these disciplines, but if not back then, college allowed us the ideal breeding grounds for our lifelong obsessions and foibles. I also realized once and for all that I loathed my stepbrother (who is also the former classmate who stole small, valuable objects from neighbors), in part because when he came to visit me at The Ohio State University during his spring break from the tonier Colgate, he flashed my roommate and me, and when we both screamed, told us with a smirk to stop being such f**king prudes because it was just a joke and didn't we know that college was supposed to be about letting it all hang out, despite the fact we had chosen lifeless and backward Columbus, on the lame eastern fringes of the boring Middle West, as the location of our coming-of-age experiences? (The previous sentence is a paraphrase, but the general tenor and meaning of his tirade has been preserved.)

- Spring semester, Sophomore year, 1990–91 - Even under penalty of tears and tantrums, do not agree to go if your roommate pleads with you to take part in a ghost-hunting expedition in downtown Columbus, not only because it is overpriced and a witless waste of time, but also because you might, to your still-great disbelief, bring an actual ghost home with you. How this happened, we weren't sure, but in fact, it did happen. For the remaining seven weeks of the semester, the mirror over the sink in the corner of our dorm room took on a cracked aspect after the hour of eleven PM, and each morning when we awoke, we'd find our underwear had been herded into the back of my roommate's closet, some of it disturbingly damp, as if worn by a profusely sweating girl-ghost. Were we being taught a lesson in the vanity of our ways? Some of the underwear was made from lace and worn solely with the intent of being flaunted before dumb boys who would not have cared if we were wearing underwear stitched from a potato sack, as long as it came off as easily as any other fabric did.

- Fall semester, Senior year, 1992–93 - "The main reason you should get a college education," Professor Randall Dixon said near the end of the semester in European History from 1900 to WWII, "which is the same reason you should study history, is to learn humility."

A student with a southern accent who had lived in my dorm freshman year, raised her hand and said, "Isn't that also the main purpose of life? Aren't we supposed to learn to bow down to the government, to our bosses and husbands and police officers and politicians, from here on out?"

Professor Dixon blinked for several long seconds before answering. He smiled and shook his head. "Submission, humility, self-abnegation, self-immolation, suicide." He paused. "Not that I'm advocating anything but humility. Still, people have killed themselves for far less than bad government and a surfeit of murderous stupidity."

A few days later, Professor Dixon was reprimanded by his department chair for this minor blip of a political protest speech, after an aggrieved student filed a complaint. It had seemed to him that his professor was advocating suicide and was probably a nihilist or maybe even a Satanist. At the time, I was dating this self-righteous idiot. His name was Mike Post and he ate chicken Kiev every Thursday and fish sticks with mashed potatoes every Friday. He had a big p*n*s and, needless to say, a small brain and heart.

- *Spring semester, Senior year, 1992–93* - When my closest friend from home, Elizabeth Perle, came to visit over her spring break, which was one week before my spring break (half of which I had planned to spend at her college), I made the mistake of having sex with my boyfriend in the same room where Elizabeth was asleep, or had been asleep until our rude noises awoke her. I didn't know that she was in the room because I had been drinking my classmate Yasmina Pujoles' "Toxic Waste Dump Punch" and stayed later at Yasmina's birthday party than Elizabeth had wanted us to, which meant that E. walked home alone, deciding as she walked the several blocks between the party and my apartment that she no longer wanted to have anything to do with me. I was a shallow, sometimes-bulimic, weekend lush who had developed an annoying laugh and a falsely breathless way of talking that she thought made me sound like a parodic Marilyn Monroe impersonator. At the time, I thought she was being prudish and mean, but after several years of calling her uncharitable names to a diminishing number of mutual friends, I finally realized that I had behaved like a self-absorbed idiot who was more interested in trying to please boys who would never really love me than maintaining the most meaningful friendship (so far) of my life.

CULTS

- *5/95–7/98* - Member, L. Ron Hubbard's Church of Scientology. Personal schism with church occurred when the suggested tithe went up by eighteen percent overnight because of roof problem that was idiot minister's own fault. He tried to create a refuge for bald eagles on top of the church by attempting to grow scrub and pine trees and installing a miniature lake and 1/100 scale model of a mountain range meant to duplicate the Canadian Rockies, which cost more than $100,000 and caused the aging roof to collapse just after a birthday party for Mr. Hubbard (who has been dead for a long time but a party is still held in his honor by many ministers each year because Mr. Hubbard is the Scientology robots' own personal Jesus figure, but without the crucifixion and loaves-and-fishes stories—just the UFOs and celebrity adherents who are so easy to brainwash it might be hilarious if it weren't also so sad).

- *2/96–present* - Member, Nicolas Cage Fan Club* - Despite a hairstyle that fluctuates between silly, seriously balding, and chic-retro-minimalist, Mr. Cage is a supreme thespian who is known for taking risks with the roles he has chosen to promulgate his genius in the world, *National Treasure* and *The Rock* notwithstanding. His early triumphs in *Valley Girl* and the tonally opposite but equally seductive *Wild at Heart* remain signal achievements in the Hollywood pantheon. The one time I was in the same place at the same time as Mr. Cage, he was chatting up an underage waitress and also seemed to be drinking a lot of sake, but he was kind enough to kiss my hand and then autograph my forearm when I introduced myself; he also winked at me with his swoon-inducing blue-green eyes.

*The Nic Cage Fan Club isn't, technically, a cult, but I can recognize that devotion to a celebrity, especially one who isn't likely ever to befriend you, more or less does put you in the same realm as cult membership.

WORK EXPERIENCE
- *September 1991–May 1993* - **The Ohio State University Bookstore**, Columbus, OH
* **Cashier**. Duties included: ringing up purchases; making change; keeping the checkout area free of trash and general debris, along with loiterers, drunks, dogs of the non–seeing-eye variety, smokers, loudly laughing people, Christmas carolers, panhandlers, and trick-or-treaters.
* Awarded Employee of the Month in April 1992, despite unfortunate clash with energetically sweating Hallmark vendor over stale chocolates the Kansas City–based company (which has since successfully diversified itself as a viable multimedia entity, though what it mainly sells is feel-good or tearjerker-type movie flotsam) had believed it could sell along with its puppy and kitten stickers and birthday and Boss's Day cards.

* Won holiday brownie bake-off for all bookstore employees, December 1991. Never admitted that half of the brownie mix was taken from a Betty Crocker box. Other key ingredients included peanut butter, mini-marshmallows, walnuts, and Bailey's Irish Cream. (Alcohol wasn't supposed to be used either.)

- *August 1993–November 1997* - **Dublin Animal Hospital**, Dublin, OH
* **Receptionist/Bookkeeper**. Not really a job related to my college degree, but I did work with money and wrote out receipts for those who paid in full after their once-carefree animals had been worked into a terrified frenzy by the two veterinarians, a husband-and-wife team who often bickered in the back rooms (a place where they thought no one in the reception area would be able to hear them), usually about who had spent how much on what useless object or who had been rude to or had leered at the other's best friend, or, would Dr. Keith ever stop stuffing his face at one in the morning and watching garbage TV until four am? He was disgusting, just disgusting, nothing like the man Dr. Kimberly had met in vet school and fallen in love with and didn't he know it was such a sad joke that he thought their neighbor's teenage daughter looked at him with anything but revulsion?

- *November 1997–July 1998* - Dublin, OH
* **Unemployed**. Minor nervous breakdown three months into unemployment stint, precipitated by two back-to-back incidents. The first: a hotel-room burglary that occurred during a weekend trip to New York City where my plan was to see as many museums and off-Broadway plays as could be squeezed into two and a half days. Was very disappointed that I could not get tickets to see Ralph Fiennes in *Hamlet*, the British actor who, for years, along with Nicolas Cage, I had the strong sense I was destined to marry. Items lost included passport, grandmother's filigreed silver locket with picture of grandfather from boyhood, laptop with compromising photos on it taken by ex-boyfriend, six pairs of underwear (three of them unwashed—the thief must have been a pervert), one small jar of peanut butter, four sheets of heart stickers and pink writing paper, one green marble calligraphy pen, one box of Ritz crackers, assorted toiletries including a big bottle of Anaïs Anaïs perfume, several tampons, one tube of Crest toothpaste (travel size), one contact case, one bottle of contact solution, one pair of toenail clippers, tweezers. The worst was that they also stole $142, money that I had borrowed from the ex-boyfriend, a guy who insisted that every cent be paid back whenever he lent me money, which he continued to do even after we broke up because he dumped me for someone else and his guilty

conscience made it difficult for him to say no when I asked for a loan, but not so difficult to demand repayment. It took me three months to pay him back because of my unemployed status. I earned a small amount of money during that time by selling my CDs and my favorite clothes (except for the Elite Prince tee shirt) on consignment at Out of the Closet.

The second: A drugged-out nutcase accosted me at a U2 concert. It's painful for me to recount the circumstances in full, but here is a short summary: I had on a new dress, one that I'd bought on sale. It was Laundry and beautiful, the kind of dress you're sure will change your life. I realize that a U2 concert is not the ideal place to wear a marvelous new dress, but I couldn't wait. The druggie/nutcase grabbed me from behind, unzipped the dress all the way down and tore it from my body in one violent motion like someone pulling a curtain from a rod. I had on a bra and a pair of underwear that didn't match and there were holes in the underwear. I don't know why I didn't bother wearing a nicer pair, considering how spectacular the dress was. People all around me started shrieking and staring when they saw me standing there in my disgraceful bikini briefs. The nutcase took off through the crowd with the dress while I cried and tried to cover my humiliating near-nakedness. My assailant was a woman, a large one with pink and blue hair. I think we might have gone to high school together, but that seems improbable now, considering the concert was in Ohio and I went to high school in Massachusetts. A well-meaning insurance salesman eventually gave me his Cincinnati Reds sweat-shirt, which I tearfully pulled on. He also gave me his address so that I could return the sweatshirt, which he said was his favorite. The one good thing about it was that it almost matched the red high heels I was wearing.

- July 1998–February 2007 - **Best Buy**, Lincoln, NE
* **Cashier** (7/98–4/00), **Assistant Manager** (4/00–3/03), **Manager** (3/03–2/07). (How on earth did I end up in Lincoln, Nebraska? Please refer to **Disasters, Averted or Otherwise**.) I think you could say, in view of my nine years' experience at this large chain-store hellhole, that I have paid my cosmic dues, whatever they might be. First, for twenty-one long months, I rang up Britney Spears and Garth Brooks and remaindered Yanni CDs, Doom video games, big-screen television sets, exorbitant-ly priced printer ink cartridges (what an effing con those things are!), cell phones, car stereos, Pilates DVDs and impulse-buy king-size Snickers bars. I called for price checks and for managers to deal with the irate, bipolar customers who were almost apoplectic when the advertised sale price did not ring up for their CD Walkmen and

jump drives and *Seinfeld*, Season 1 DVDs. I learned so much about human nature that I am now as qualified as your favorite therapist to counsel the disenchanted, the lonely and distraught, the beaten-down, the oblivious, the bankrupt/shopping-addicted, the selfish, and the foolish.

I was looking for other jobs—consulting, human resources, accounting, hospitality industry, etc.—while cashiering, but no one was hiring. At least not me.

Wearing the **Assistant Manager** crown was slightly better. I got a few days of paid vacation every year, marginal health insurance, slight respect from the nicer customers, and the scornful envy of my former peers (those cashiers who were deemed unpromotable). Lessons learned or relearned included, but were not limited to:

a) Elderly churchgoers are as likely to shoplift as meth-addicted teenagers.

b) No one has any respect for the break room's cleanliness, no matter their rank and salary; the same for the restrooms.

c) A pregnant woman might actually be a creative thief with a picnic basket concealed beneath her blouse instead of a burgeoning fetus, one she has filled to the brim with CDs and DVDs.

d) The supervisor's children and wife are, as a rule, spawn of Satan (which I guess makes the supervisor Satan).

I was promoted to **Manager of Entertainment Media** (a pretentious name for music and movies) because of the kindness of the supervisor who had two young children who were known for torturing household pets and pilfering coins and small bills from their parents' and their aunts' and uncles' wallets. I fell hard for this supervisor, despite his tendency to do bad Adam Sandler impressions and compulsively eat powdered doughnuts that left a fine sugar dust on his goatee. Needless to say, this seminal love affair did not end the way I hoped it would, and I soon left Best Buy for my next employer (details immediately below). I couldn't bear to look at the supervisor any longer, because I kept imagining him in the throes of orgasm, which made me feel maudlin on some days, horny on others. This faithless, doughnut-addicted man is, as far as I know, still married to his chronically unpleasant wife, and likely will spend the rest of his life bailing his ingrate children out of one scrape after another, some of these scrapes financial, some of them personal and sordid, a few of them, most likely, criminal.

- *March 2007–December 2009* - **Dogs in Suds**, Winfield, NE

* **Manager/Dog Groomer**. It is an open secret that once a dog falls for you, she will love you unconditionally until her death (provided you don't mistreat her—a crime that would earn you a place in hell with the rapists and serial killers, I'm absolutely certain). I loved this job, and the only reason it ended in December of 2009 was because we went out of business. We had a problem with a big dumb Labrador retriever attacking an aging, asthmatic poodle, and word traveled in its predictable trajectory: bad news flies/ricochets/exists in an eternal vacuum, ready to resurface at any time, whereas this dog beauty parlor of the first order had previously enjoyed a flawless reputation—ten years of solid business practices and solvency with devoted clients, its owner (Mimi Hart) the founder and annual sponsor of the Doggy Day Parade down Cherry Street and a generous donor to local animal shelters where we went twice a year to give bubble and flea baths to the canine inmates, providing each grateful dog with his/her very own flea collar.

One of the few things I didn't like about this job was some of the dog owners: wealthy sourpusses who had had disastrous nose jobs in some cases, very noticeable breast augmentation surgery in others, or both. Not like there's anything wrong with plastic surgery (if you can afford it), but just because you have a snub nose and huge tits doesn't make you God's Gift to the Universe, Elisha H.!

Since Dogs in Suds went out of business, I have been temping for Crème of the Crop, doing secretarial work for ConAgra, mostly. I've found that after nearly two years of grooming and bathing dogs, cute as they are, it's nice to see men in suits again. Some of these professional guys smell of onions, others of talcum powder; some compulsively check their cell phones for texts (from mistresses?); one or two unaccountably have tears in their eyes when they think no one is looking. I want to take these sad, well-groomed men into my arms and offer them solace but am not sure how such a gesture would be interpreted.

IRRATIONAL FEARS
* Cobras (with hoods unfurled to their full glory; even typing this makes me feel anxious and lightheaded)
* Seagull attacks
* Being killed with piano wire (a type of grisly choking death often used in violent movies, especially those of the '80s and '90s)
* Decapitation by a window falling from a skyscraper or a helicopter blade that flies off of a traffic helicopter and goes scissoring through the air to find me as I walk to the library or to the convenience store for chocolate

* The one week I don't play Mega Millions, my numbers are chosen (therefore, I always play)

SEMI-RATIONAL FEARS
* Rape
* Poverty
* Car crashes
* Food poisoning (especially in burrito huts, McDonald's, and roadside bratwurst stands in small Wisconsin towns, including the one where my maternal grandmother lives)
* Identity theft
* Rabid squirrels, skunks, opossums, dogs, porcupines, armadillos, bats, cats, raccoons, mice, rats, shrews, chipmunks, ferrets, cows, sheep, bulls, llamas
* My parents' deaths
* My friends' deaths
* Dying alone and childless, incontinent, senile, and unloved
* Decapitation by the eighteenth-century guillotine on display in the Weapons of War and Instruments of Torture Museum in the Wisconsin town where my maternal grandmother lives. Guillotine blade has, on two separate occasions, fallen down with a terrifying, vengeful *whhaapp!* while alarmed visitors looked on. The docent pleaded innocent to this mischief but could not stop laughing at the looks on her tour group's faces.

DISASTERS, AVERTED OR OTHERWISE
- Early August 1991 - **Motorcycle ride** with Poe Wilczek, sophomore-year college crush. Poe hit a dead opossum in the road, slammed on the brakes, and sent us both flying into a drainage ditch. I was wearing jeans, a leather jacket, and a helmet and was all right, aside from about five hundred bruises and a chipped tooth; Poe was wearing a helmet too but had on shorts and a tee shirt. Needless to say, his arms and legs and back looked like someone had gone after him with a cheese grater, but his brains were still intact. So to speak.

- May 1993 - **Move to Los Angeles** to try to break into the movie business contemplated then decided against

- *May 1993* - **Move to New York City** to try to break into Broadway musicals contemplated then decided against

- *May 1993–April 1998* - **Minor disasters**:
a) an adoption of a feral (?) cat (shelter worker didn't mention how numerous and scary this cat's problems were; cat was returned and probably, sad to say, sent into the next life in short order)
b) feather instead of foam pillows at a B and B in Wheeling, West Virginia
c) a collision with a deer while riding in Rich Dolzer's Ford Fiesta after a pool party while visiting college friends in Indianapolis
d) the theft of my purse at a Dublin, Ohio, strip mall (but **overall**, these five years were **fairly tranquil**)

- *April 1998* - **Engagement** to Jesse Cates called off in favor of a relationship with Mitchell Cates (Jesse's cousin), which resulted in Mitch's and my abrupt departure for Lincoln, Nebraska, where Mitch had lined up a job at the University of Nebraska's bursar's office.

- *December 1998* - **Mitch dumps me for idiot** named Courtney Foster who has big boobs, a fat ass, and a snorting laugh that for several years appeared in my nightmares. Her dad is loaded and she doesn't have to work, so she doesn't. When I knew her, she used to go around saying, "The world isn't as bad a place as some people who write for big-time newspapers would like us to think." Also, "New York City is the root of all evil." But instead of saying "root," she said it "rout," as in, "That army routed its enemies."

* **Fast-forward to near-death experience**:
- *March 2010* - A **road trip** to Arches National Park and the Grand Canyon with my friend Jane Garcia who worked with me at Dogs in Suds. We were parked at an overlook at Arches when a carload of teenagers wearing tee shirts with the names of pro football teams on them showed up and dumped an ashtray of butts out the window next to our car. I was in a **rotten mood** because my stepbrother had just texted me to say that he needed to borrow $300 again (for some reeking dive's video poker machines, probably, or else to give to his **lame-ass girlfriend** who has cheated on him with at least two different guys). I picked up a handful of

the discarded butts, some of them soggy, and threw them at the windshield of the teenagers' car, yelling, more or less, "Go eff yourselves. This is a national park. Can't you show some effing decency for once in your worthless lives?"

This did not go over well. Jane was still in the car, and she rolled up the windows and locked the doors, not realizing, I don't think, that I couldn't get back in now. Two of the teenagers, **miscreants** who looked like they each weighed twice as much as I did, picked me up like a suitcase (their friends drunk and laughing and shouting behind us) and carried me to the edge of the overlook, threatening to pitch me down the billion-year old rock bed to my **probable death**. I looked down toward my last moments and said, I'm not sure why, "If you let me live, I promise never to tell another lie." They laughed like I was insane but stepped back from the ledge. They took me back to my car, dropped me on my knees hard, and told me to get the eff out of their faces, crazy-a** b*tch!

Needless to say, my vow not to tell any more lies led me to my idea that a cover letter and resume shouldn't contain any lies either. Hence this revolutionary (?) job application that you hold in your hands (or else are reading on your computer screen).

EXTRACURRICULAR INTERESTS

Books - I am not a devoted, surly fan of *Catcher in the Rye* or any books about vampires, wizards, baseball, or ones that involve people transformed into insects upon waking.

- I greatly admire *Lolita* because I think V. Nabokov was a genius, if not also a bit of a pervert, but this isn't really a big deal. I think we all have a pervert strain in us, whether we like it or not. And Nabokov was Russian, so what can we expect, considering how messed up Russia's history is, with its many maniacs of yore in high places, endless winters, enormous vodka dependency?

Movies - *Leaving Las Vegas* (for which Mr. Cage won the Best Actor Oscar!), *Wild at Heart, Valley Girl, Bad Lieutenant: Port of Call New Orleans*
- *The English Patient* (for which Mr. Fiennes should have won the Best Actor Oscar!)
- *Monsters Inc.* (This remains the best kids' movie around, even better than *Old Yeller*, and of course much different.)
- *Butch Cassidy and the Sundance Kid* (Paul Newman was originally considered for the role of Sundance. How our history would have been different if he had been cast as the sidekick instead of the man with all the [sometimes wrong] answers!)

- *The Graduate* (Every woman, after a certain age, has a bit of Mrs. Robinson in her. Like Nabokov's pervert strain, there's nothing wrong with this either.)

Music* - Nothing country, please. I cannot deal, except I do like the sound of the banjo, which is a comical-looking instrument, but jaunty and stylish in sound. I also admire Gillian Welch, though she's more cerebral and bluegrass-esque, which isn't nearly as offensive as the dreck played on the low-rent radio stations scattered across the US like pimples on the greasy face of an adolescent boy, one who hasn't had a fresh, uncooked vegetable since he was five, or possibly ever.
- Anything by Prince, pre-1993 - e.g. *Purple Rain, Parade, Around the World in a Day, 1999, Controversy, Dirty Mind, For You, Prince*
- David Bowie (pronounced Bo-ee, not Bow-ee, as in bow-wow-wow) - *Let's Dance, Tonight*
- Duran Duran's *Greatest Hits*
- Peter Gabriel's perfect *So*
- Rick Springfield's *Success Hasn't Spoiled Me Yet* ("Jessie's Girl" is just fine, but who could forget the barely contained jealousy of "Don't Talk to Strangers"?)
- Robert Palmer's *Riptide* (Everyone must remember the insistent, almost lunatic beat of "Addicted to Love," not to mention the music video with its clonelike brown-haired babes in tight black dresses.)

*You probably have noticed a pattern here. The '80s was a musically rich and diverse period, if not the most morally exemplary time in our country's history.

References Usually Available Upon Request

SAMPLE INTERVIEW QUESTIONS:

1. If you are being charged by a wild boar, and at the same time, only a few yards away, your domestic partner and/or best friend is being charged by a rabid raccoon, what would you do?

2. If you found a wallet that contained a few hundred dollars in cash and the driver's license inside revealed that the wallet belonged to a former mean-spirited neighbor who had ruthlessly clashed with you and/or your family for years, would you return the wallet? Yes or no. Please explain your rationale.

3. If you witnessed a coworker you like and respect doing something illegal outside of the workplace such as shoplifting condoms, or mistreating a small, defenseless animal (e.g. a declawed cat or a hamster), what would you do?

4. The same scenario as above but the coworker is one you do not like and respect.

5. Do you listen to country music? Yes or no. Please explain.

6. If reincarnation were real and you had to choose to return in your next life as one of the following, which would it be and why?
   a) lion
   b) grizzly bear
   c) panda bear
   d) skunk
   e) Tennessee Williams
   f) cockroach

7. Free-association exercise: What image or thought first comes to mind after you hear each of the following words?
   a) construction zone
   b) prostate gland
   c) thief
   d) spendthrift
   e) playboy
   f) tits

8. Have you ever wanted to assassinate one of our presidents, congresspeople, or senators? Yes or no. Please explain.

9. If you were told that you'd have to eat one serving of the following at each meal, every single day for the rest of your life, which would you choose?
   a) black licorice
   b) Snickers bar
   c) mushrooms (sautéed)
   d) beef jerky
   e) Bosc pear
   f) corn curls

Dennis Hinrichsen
Every Coral Branch Supports the Moon

ANSWER TO A ZEN KOAN / FOR MY MOTHER

There was a river in her head that kept flowing
And so she

Sang
At a piano built

From air,

Hands
Frail and spotted with match-heads.

Strange singer she was,

Mask
Forcing pressure

Into a failing heart
So the external lung that kept pumping

Was nearly opera

In the room, grand, scaled—
La Scala—

And the chambers of her dying

Its box
And voice.

But no sound came. Plank
On plank

She kept building,

Reaching out,
Leaning,

Bridging some lumber in her head

With deeper wood.
I thought fear

Would take her
Like some Jesus bucket

Tearing

At the bottom of a well
When the preacher

Gripped her skull

And uttered last harsh words,
But it was she

Who came to drink,
Not some savior

In the shape

Of a man's palm.
And so I too sucked breath

In hospital light,

Brought her dripping
From the sea.

Gave her a "cup of winter,"
Language

Having clotted in a sheath of thought—

A particle
Of ice—

It was all she could whisper,

Dying,
To get a glass of cooling tea.

Mother,
It was morphine.

I let them wand your heart

To disconnect it,
And then we pumped the slurry in.

Nobody winced

Because it was beautiful and smooth,
A fat,

Controllable lightning,
Cured

With honey.

How it serenely sleeved the wires of your brain,
The nerves,

The cheekbones I saw yellowed

With jaundice,
That Taj Mahal of heresy and belief

We call the self
Come crashing down,

Zone

By zone, reduced,
Surrendered

To one thin hand caressing your cold dead leg.

Skin Music: a memoir

After 40 years I still wonder about the carp and our neighbor. Whatever possessed him to spend all that time catching a creel's-worth of bottom feeders, cleaning, filleting, breading, deep-frying, then walking down the alley in time for our dinner, saying he'd cooked us some catfish.

We often ate catfish we caught from the river so it seemed right.

It was a gift, summer's
      bounty, the plate
   something

      he'd fashioned
 from crimped
   aluminum foil . . .

And so we said our thanks and ate, completing the joke.

I will never understand it. Was it a dig at my father—his subtle arrogance—despite four kids and a lousy job? Were they drinking buddies? My father took his accordion up there sometimes and played unhinged polkas on Saturday nights.

I think now his point was Shakespearean, vicious. The man's cruel knowledge, our blindness, that he was eating the neighborhood children.

The carp was their flesh.

*

In retrospect the strategies were astounding. For the adults first—win their hearts—the man built a horseshoe pit and badminton court in the schoolyard across the alley.

        Long into dusk the shuttlecock
                whirred, the horseshoes
           clanged and spun.

Afterwards, gin and tonics, cigarettes, laughter, talk, 8 mm cartoons he sometimes ran backwards.

In the yard, a set of bars, high and low, a child could hang from, arms stretched out, pure orangutan,

        or swing from the knees,
                sundress sailing.

And then in a stroke of brilliance on that 20 x 40 lot he buried coffee cans for miniature golf, all 18 holes, front to back.

He even let the children paint the side of his house with water. Hours they spent brushing in sunlight, letting it dry, repainting in long strokes what seemed a jungle—the house was green.

   This was hunting season, exquisite patience.

      The days unwinding, heating up,
                  the hedges coming
            unlatched until

a lone child appeared.

                              *

      It comes out later that you want to kill somebody that's
already dead—

         a brother's 17, still wetting
               the sheets, it's
            a sister's wedding day—and

then suddenly you're in a car with baseball bats and hammers heading for that old block.

Your grandfather wants to drive a 9-inch nail into the man's heart, but the man's dead so you just circle, up D Avenue shouting his name, and then down the alley, back again.

Thinking what next.

Thinking how brazen the bastard was, lazy in a way, disciplined—it was his own block—

> whispering some germ of fear,
>   self-poison, into
>   a child's ear before

he pulled the kid's pants down.

That secret voice, part man, part boy or girl, like wet shoelace, double-looped, frozen.

No matter how you move, alone, in another's arms, it won't unknot.

*

8 or 9 at the time, I was too old for him.

I owned jackknives, pubic hair, a fishing pole.

Had an arch enemy the next house over, Carroll Stephen Luckey the 3rd—how perfect was that—we, the Blakeslee boys and I, tried to drown once and who later shot at us from his roof with a pellet gun because we teased him when he cleaned his hamster cage and stuffed the two creatures like a pair of mittens into a mason jar—to protect them—then closed the lid . . .

We had hydrochloric acid,
                              wrist-rockets we'd
              built from hangers,

Schwinn bikes. Every dime we begged or stole

        we'd spend on candy, Ohio
                      Blue Tips, then
              ride to the slough,

try to set ourselves, the world, on fire.
        Zipper, stretched jeans, dirty nail, it didn't matter.
        We were covered in scabs, waved to the child molester as we angled past him, perfect in our bodies, throwing stones, cussing, on our way to the movies burning with other idle men.

*

And then it was night.

Temperature and wind overlaid the scattered pools of human skin until it was one water ghosting the alley.

        Carroll Stephen Luckey the 2nd
                finally able
           to screw his wife, now

his son was sleeping, and those rude boys who earlier had thrown dirt clods against his upstairs window as he tried to slowly disrobe her—

        beautiful,
                lovely
           shadowplay—

had gone home to their nightly beatings.

The youngest children asleep in their pods of covers, post-invasion, bodies snatched, building sad alien selves.

The child molester wide awake two houses over in a second storey room,

terrified of winter
              and
     empty yards.

His body as still as the elaborate train set he'd built in his basement.
Dust settling everywhere.
On the families disembarking, the delicate signs, the false eye of the engine.

*

I saw my first naked girl
             that year,
     a Blakeslee daughter.

The boys had drilled holes in the plywood wall between the bedrooms so when she showered that June day we raced ahead and waited for her to dress.

Three eyes to three holes, two brothers, neighbor, all idiots, the girl stretching, unaware, like Athena in the mirror.

I remember the whiteness of her belly,

the just budding nipples,
faint,
pink, and

was lost in how quiet
her
gaze was. My own gaze

part skin, part music, reefing a shore I could barely imagine.
And then the spell broke.
She dressed and was dork girl again, sheathed in innocence.
Numbed, altered, torqued, I looked for my bike, loaded pole and matches,
lures and bait, headed for the creek.

It was summer, always high
summer,
in that blistered world.

I caught fish.
Old enough to get fucked in the ass, or suck a derelict's dick, I thought of that
girl immaculate before the mirror, then put my knife to the gill.

Drown

Fraudulent river, how can
I believe anything you
say? I walk past nine trees, see
a bird, and then that one man
fishing at the edge of vision is floating by. I can't
see the body at first so
I think his waders are the
trousers of the Lord swelled with
run-off and velocity
from the dam. But they are not.
I don't wade in. The others
with me don't wade in. We just
stroll along, watch the trousers
betray the current through a
flock of un-nerved ducks. It is
only when I call to the
fishermen paddling by to
touch a heel and they recoil
that I sense the heaviness
you carry. Fat man on a
graying Sunday dead of a

busted vein or bubble in
in the heart so his body
caved and his garments filled and
he was flannelled thrashing in
waist-deep water. Somebody
must have called from the dam, then
leaned back, fishing. Smoked above
the whirlpools and raw-toothed flail-
ing until the river was
gentle and flat. I am on
the bridge when they pull him out,
so much spilling from his face
I think he is the source of
molten silver. Eyes wide o-
pen. Packed with stone. Because that's
what you are, river, stone lung
and stone heart they try to beat
to life again with useless
hands. Body hauled—such important fury—from a yellow
rubber boat to the anvil
of a rotted dock I think

a living blade might be forged
fist by fist. My fist if I'd
waded in. My lips two sparks
to ignite a cough. Or whatever that stutter is when
the dying gasp and fountain
unrepentant river to
the streaming earth. I wait. No
such breath forthcomes. No such birth.
Just spidery rush-off—ech-
o of a man. How can I
believe anything it says?

Rachel May
Avery

Touch.

Soaked through, Avery came in from the rain. We told him, when we saw him coming, that we didn't want him here. We even said it in really loud voices: "Avery! We DON'T WANT YOU HERE!" We screamed it from the deck, up on the hill, and we leaned over the deck, and we said it until our voices were hoarse and our heads were all wet from sticking them out in the rain and our stomachs hurt from the top rail pressing into us. But maybe he couldn't hear us. Or maybe he could and he was just so sad that he ignored us, and kept on coming. We knew he had nowhere else to go. He was Avery, skinny and slouched and always alone. Poor Avery. With his hood over his head. His big shoes. He always wore his brother's shoes, hand-me-downs, two sizes too big, and by the time he grew into them, he'd worn through the soles. So he had to switch up to the next pair. His brother was luckier than him; his brother grew so fast that he got new shoes every few months, and his shoes never wore out, and they always fit right. But if Avery wasn't ready for a pair yet, they were passed onto his cousins, who were, and so Avery always got his brother's just-too-small shoes, and the not the several-pairs-ago-pair that might have fit. No one really knew why Avery was sad, why he slouched, why he was skinny, why he had black pools around his eyes underneath his skin, like that's where he was storing all the sadness. No one knew because he didn't talk, and that's why we didn't like him. We didn't like people who slouched and wouldn't explain why. We wanted to know the reason. We wanted to know what was his story, please. When we yelled at Avery, he didn't respond, and that made us more adamant. He should've known by now. He really should've. When he came up onto the deck, his shoes went klomp, klomp, klomp, and they made a squishing sound as his foot lifted up. Klomp-shhhhh! Klomp-shhhh! Like his foot was pulling up all the water in the soles. He walked onto the porch and Agatha said, "What the heck, Avery? We said no Averies here."

Our uncles painted this deck blue three years ago, and then they went out to sea to catch some lobsters and died. Now our mother won't repaint the deck because she doesn't want to cover up any memories of her brothers.

And Avery looked down at her, and pinched his eyebrows together, and frowned in a way that looked like it was supposed to be a smile. He pulled his hood from his head and let the water drip off the hood and down his back. It splattered onto the backs of his calves, onto the blue deck. Our uncles painted this deck blue three years ago, and then they went out to sea to catch some lobsters and died. Now our mother won't repaint the deck because she doesn't want to cover up any memories of her brothers, she says. "Yeah," said Thomas, "get off, Avery," and Thomas walked forward and tried to look menacing. I saw him practicing this look in the mirror the other day, and making a little growling sound. Avery leaned back, toward the long set of stairs that led back down to the street, where it was still raining. The rain made a sound like a river all around us. "Maybe he can stay," I said. "Maybe it doesn't matter too much." I didn't want Avery to fall down the stairs. I didn't want him to cry. His face was balling up into more and more of a grimace, or a look of consternation, as if he was on the verge and soon he would erupt. And when he erupted, he would melt, right here on our deck, into pools of black sadness like the pools underneath his eyes—it would all slip out from his body, at last, and we would see what a sack of sorrow he was, and wonder how he had held it all together for so long, anyway, with just the skin to cover the sorrow. So much of it. Just underneath. How he had even managed to move his legs and his arms and keep his neck up straight. That's what I saw, then, finally, after so much time of hollering at him—and maybe I had always seen it but I was afraid, and yelling was easier. It was what Thomas did. Agatha and I, we always did what Thomas did. Avery cleared his throat. It made a sound like a robin chirping. We thought, Here it comes, he'll speak. We waited. Later, we'd talk about how long we waited for him to talk, as if the rain stretched the moment into days and days. How our parents never guessed, when we went inside, that a lifetime had passed out on the deck. There they were, reading the paper and watching TV, my father's ankles crossed and my mother's tucked underneath her, and they didn't even realize the whole world had gone by. Avery opened his mouth. Avery closed his mouth. We all just watched. Finally, after a long time of just listening to the rain and watching Avery very closely, Thomas said, "WHAT? WHAT? You're making us CRAZY, AVERY!!" And that made Agatha move closer, too, almost close enough to touch Avery. But she wasn't yelling anymore. She had her finger in her mouth. She is the youngest of us all, the most curious, the most likely to laugh. Avery kept opening and closing his mouth, and Thomas said, "Goldfish! Goldfish!" and puckered up his lips and copied Avery, turned his arms into fins, bent at the elbow with his hands underneath his armpits, and flapped them back and forth. Wiggled his butt as if it was a tail. Raised and lowered his head like he was diving. And Avery couldn't stop opening and closing his mouth. He was stuck, I could see, stuck in this motion, and the more Thomas mocked him, the more Avery was stuck, the more upset he looked, his eyebrows just one brow now, tears sliding down his cheeks, his mouth opening and closing and opening and closing, until it hurt me to watch, until it felt as if someone was yanking my own jaw open and closed and opened and closed, and pressing very hard on the part of me that hurt the most—the being-afraid-of-the-dark-part, the time-I-got-lost-at-the-fair-and-no-one-noticed-for-hours part—and I felt as if it was all slipping from somewhere inside me, up to my jaw, and back again, a big loop, a big loop of stuck. "Stop that," I said. First it was very quiet, and no one heard. And Thomas kept doing it, and Avery kept doing what he was doing, and I said it again, very loud: "STOP THAT! STOP IT STOP IT STOP IT!" and I threw my hands in the air and stomped my feet and let myself wail. I let out everything, all at once. I spit out the carousel that I'd watched for an hour and the sheep that I'd sat beside while I watched all the strangers who weren't my parents walk past, and I'd wondered if I'd ever have a family again, and I spit out the nights I woke up most afraid and screamed for my mother to help me but she didn't come, maybe because I was screaming silent—those times you're so afraid your voice doesn't come out—or because she didn't hear or she didn't want to get out of bed, I don't know; I only know she didn't come, and I was so afraid, too afraid to get out of bed and walk down the hall and find her, so I could only cry myself to sleep. Thomas laughed, and looked at Avery and said, "Yeah!" And I got quiet, then, and

I looked straight at Thomas, and I said, "No, you. YOU, Thomas, you stop." And I pointed at him, and I even leaned forward and let my finger almost touch his shoulder, like I might push if he provoked me, like I wasn't scared at all. He was wearing his orange striped shirt. And he turned to me and looked at me with his own jaw open, like he couldn't believe what I had done, and the rain kept falling, and Agatha watched us with her finger in her mouth, her black hair all frizzy around her face like it always is in the rain. I stared at Thomas. He put his arms down. He closed his mouth. He looked back at me, and when he did, I saw he was ashamed. It was the first time I ever saw him look that way. Agatha turned to Avery. I tried to catch my breath, my chest going up and down, my heart beating fastfastfast, because I was so afraid just then, doing what I'd never had the courage to do before. And it had worked. And I was stunned. I saw, out of the corner of my eye, Agatha, who reached out to touch Avery. She pressed her hand to his jaw, and let it stay there. It was a reach for her, to get to his jaw. I turned to watch. He closed his mouth. He kept his eyes on us, but he could feel her, we knew. We all just breathed. And when his mouth was closed, his eyebrows relaxed into their natural place on his forehead, and all the muscles in his face relaxed, and then there was this miracle, and his lips turned up.

Susan White Norman
Casco on the Foam Planet

My girlfriend eats with a good appetite, but she's still skinny. Char's Puerto Rican skinny and that means round in the right places. Last spring, she started calling me Casco. This is Spanish for helmet. I had to look it up. At first I refused to respond, but I'm no longer capable of unflagging resolutions, so I gave in and let Char rename me. I'm watching her eat hospital cafeteria lasagna and her jaw is clicking on one side. I sense impending reproach because my own lasagna is still untouched, an orderly tower of carbohydrates and proteins. I squeeze my helmet, which is under the table, hugged up between my calves. Sweet comfort. Momentary relief. It's really as simple as that.

The hospital's been newly renovated, and it's overly confident now with its sparse Scandinavian furniture and brilliant sunlight. I liked it better the way it was before, equal parts wood and crumbling composite tiles. A touch ominous. It wasn't nearly so sure of anything back then. This hospital was built before people came into hospitals expecting guarantees. Back then, a patient diagnosed with something as common as an irregular heartbeat would glumly accept his protracted death sentence and go along his way. His doctor might have said something like: "Sorry, old sport. It's just sour luck is all. Nothing more to be done here."

Now we can fix that in under an hour, outpatient. These days it's all glass and light and sleek consulting rooms and lasers fixing people lickity-split. Not me, though. Not even a place with windows like this is going to be able to save me.

An Asian doctor I vaguely recognize pointed at me earlier. I'm sure I've heard "Dr. Witherspoon"—my long abandoned appellation—said somewhere in this lobby, which is proving itself capable of impossible sound trajectories. I interned here, completed half a residency here, and fully projected myself out into a future of always being here. And here I am. I've been a patient in the cardio-thoracic research unit of this hospital for over a year now. Last month, I had my heart fitted with a hotshot device that a group of hotshots designed just for me. Though not as I'd envisioned, which was as an attending surgical resident with a house out of town and a condo in the city, I'm still here. Today I'm having lunch with my girlfriend who *is* an attending surgeon.

Char was right in the middle of it, talking to him in her calm, sultry voice. The paramedics tried to corner him while the rest of us milk babies skirted the chaos in an ever-widening circle.

There's a foursome of dermatology residents seated to our right, talking in mumbles. I think I remember the tall one from med school. "Bird-ass" we called him. I catch his eye and wave. He does the compulsory look-around before returning my wave with his chicken-wing arm.

"No one is paying any attention to you, Casco," Char says. "You do not even *know* that man. Eat your lunch." She shakes her head, and I can tell she feels bad for being sharp, but old habits die hard.

Char's stayed with me. I'm not sure why because she deserves better. Back in Puerto Rico, Char says she ate rice and beans and papaya all day and stood around in the sunshine drinking and dancing. At least, that's what she says when she's feeling homesick. Other times, she makes it sound like *Thunderdome* and it kills me. She was the last of five kids in a poor family, and the one girl, and somehow made it to college then to medical school where I met her. She says it's because she had one good aunt. Char had one worthwhile person in her sad, shitty corner back in San Juan and look what she did with it. Almost every other doctor in here floated in on the opportunity parade, waving their little flags of privilege. I know I did.

She chews slowly and makes little circles with her head, eyes closed like she'd do when I was inside her. Back when we still had sex. Ah, and we were epic. Two seemingly perfect bodies in coitus simpatico.

I shouldn't be able to get it up anymore because of the meds that are slowing down my heart, or more accurately, slowing down my blood. Less pump, pump, pump for the extremities. The thing is, I can. My function is one hundred percent in that department, confirmed most recently by a hurried self-encounter in the shower.

I was diagnosed over a year ago with an inoperable anchor protein mutation—a true rarity. I've been taking the heart meds since then and therefore lying to Char since then. As for sex, one could say I've become more giving. Extremely giving.

She suddenly looks up. "Why are you staring at me?" she says. "This is called *eating*. It's wonderful. You should try it."

I'm fully loaded now from watching her roll her head around, and I wish I could take her back to our apartment and make love to her, but I can't. I'm terrified I'd die on top of her, which would be, I think, the single worst way for me to die. Even so, the blood that's currently rushing to my dick is making me faint. I think about reaching for my helmet. Instead, I duck my head under the table and have a quick look at it.

"What are you looking for Alex, *eh*?" Char asks after she swallows. "You should eat something. You rode the train all this way to be with me at lunch, and either you're under the table or staring at me the whole time." She shakes her head again. "You're all messed up, baby. You need to eat something, and you need to get some *sleep*." I want to get up and leave because I'm sure she's going to start hassling me about missing my post-op with Dr. Crotch, but my train is still twenty minutes out.

"I'm not messed up. I'm peachy," I say. "I'm just not hungry."

Let's put things into perspective. When I was a surgical resident, I was as close to the male physical ideal as you're going to find. But that was over a year ago when I was working out four days a week, not to mention walking thirty-six holes of golf when I could fit it in. Now I weigh 155. I weighed 155 in the ninth grade.

When we first met, as interns, Charla Santos was making noodles on a hot plate and stomping roaches in her walk-up across from the Thirty-fifth Street el stop. Even so, Char walked around this hospital like displaced royalty. The women avoided her. The men were obsessed with her, and in return, she hated our asses.

"All you men are like children here in this hospital," she'd announced one day, head down, scribbling in her notebook, compelling every man within twenty feet of her to study his shoes. "Milk babies," she said before sauntering off, obscenely hot in her purple scrubs.

It's true she's fearless, and she never complains, which the rest of us did incessantly. And so in an attempt to impress her, I resolved to be more like her. There were times when this was asking too much. For example we were all, with the exception of Char, scared shitless the day a guy came into the ER in a mad panic with a butcher's knife nearly shucking his skull in two. Char was right in the middle of it, talking to him in her calm, sultry voice. The paramedics tried to corner him while the rest of us milk babies skirted the chaos in an ever-widening circle. It was Char who eventually got him to the ground, holding him across her lap, calming him like a child as he wept.

Through persistence, I eventually triumphed and Char deemed me the best of the *bebés de la leche*. Ultimately though, I like to think it came down to attraction. Attraction like ours was a chemical brain bath, a mythical soup that could never be analyzed or replicated: the perfect balance of adrenaline, dopamine, and serotonin.

Char stands up. "Have this your way, Casco," she says. "Starve for all I care." She doesn't mean it. She cares. I can see it in her buttery brown eyes.

Her belly button is winking through a gauzy, white tee shirt as she collects her things from the table. Sunlight's flooding in from the glass ceiling six floors up, and it's gathered around her. Char's a golden angel. She's pulling her long brown hair up behind her head and using it to tie a knot that looks like a cinnamon bun.

"Should I take you home and put you to bed myself?" she asks. She's arching her eyebrows, her trademark seduction. She licks into the corners of her mouth. It's too much. A thick, noodly strand falls from her bun and glides along her collarbone. I want to take her hair into my mouth and suck it. I want to twist it around my tongue. Instead, I shake my head.

"No," I whisper.

She looks at me. A clear, bottomless stare. She's considering me now and, as it goes these days, I'm overcome with directionless dread.

"I can't come home with you, Casco. I just wanted you to want me and now I'm disappointed," she says. "Besides, I've got surgery." She pulls on her lab coat, but I can see she's not ready to leave. She's looking for something else, so I pull her in around the waist and bury my face in her taut middle. I tug at the drawstring of her scrub pants with my teeth. Char lets out a pleasant moan.

"Why don't the interns eat down here anymore?" I ask through clenched teeth, biting down on a nubbin of drawstring. "It's the intern place."

"No, baby. It was *our* place," she says, pouting down at me. "The interns now don't stick together like we all once did. One will be telling something on the other one to me like this all day long. They're vicious fuckers." Her accent. It still slays me.

"Huh." I don't give a shit where the interns eat or what they do. My heart is racing. The blood, pumping at a hare's pace despite my meds, is circling down south in a closed circuit. I grab my helmet off the floor and stand up.

"Baby, *please* do not put the helmet on in here. You don't need to wear it all the time, Alex. Just hold on to it until you get out of the building, okay?" She's looking around.

Char thinks the helmet is ridiculous. She's a surgeon with an ass like two scoops of chocolate ice cream, and I'm not a surgeon anymore. I'm not even a practicing physician. I work the counter at a bookstore, and now I wear a helmet just about full-time.

What Char finds most irrational is that I chose not to take up another residency, podiatry or something equally inferior, after they pulled me from surgical because of my heart. But she feels the same way I do about surgery, so she of all people should understand. It's the precision. On our best days, we can perform acts of true and mostly irreversible correction. The other disciplines are just a few generations removed from alchemy. I can't imagine myself immersed in a life of constant speculation and questionable chemistry.

> **She looks at me. A clear bottomless stare. She's considering me now and, as it goes these days, I'm overcome with dread.**

Char reaches out to hug me and her beeper goes off. "This is the one I was waiting for. Kiss me, Casco," she says. Char turns her cheek to me, and I kiss the two little moon-shaped scars on her cheekbone. She's told me that, back in Puerto Rico, her brothers trained the dog to bite her when she'd refuse to steal for them.

Although not something I'd really considered before now, Char's cheek depresses me. I imagine her there in Puerto Rico before I knew her, tiny Char all skinny and poor and at the mercy of her sweaty gangster brothers. I never knew that loving someone would mean feeling responsible for shit that happened before you'd even met.

She suddenly takes my hand. "I've been practicing this all morning, watch. The Lima stitches." She's mimicking a pericardial stitch in my palm. I pull away, and Char pretends not to notice. "Alex, you would've loved it. Stovall threw Peters out of the OR last week after he buried the stitches on this woman and she began a retro-mediastinal bleed . . . ."

"Char, no shoptalk. I'm not your guy," I say. She looks disproportionately hurt by this.

"No, Casco," Char says. "No, you're not." She says this last part with carefully measured drama. She's walking away now.

"I got to dip, anyway," I yell after her. The lobby returns my voice to me from all sides. "I'm taking the twinks to the park to see their dad."

She turns back around. "What is this you are saying now, 'dip'?" She grabs me by the waistband, hard. There's plenty of room in there since I haven't gotten around to buying anything to fit my newly shrunken body. "You're like a skinny kid now, saying skinny kid things." She's still smiling at me. "Kiss the twins," she says and then Char leaves me, holding my blue medical helmet over my dick.

I've just put my helmet on when I see Dr. Crotch and his buddies coming across the lobby toward me. They see me. They need me. Their need compels them to tilt forward as they walk. Crotch and crew are probably going to make the *Journal* on my account.

"Alex!" Crotch yells in his authoritative bark.

I've missed my post-op, and I still haven't signed his release form. The form that allows him to publish his findings after my heart supernovas and he's rescued me with his brilliant implant. Of course, he's not sure what kind of state I'll be in after the so-called rescue, so he wants my signature up front. I don't blame him. It's going to be a mess. It's the reason I wear the helmet.

My sister Georgia's heart failed her eighteen months ago. There she was, pulling her twins up two flights of stairs in their south-side walk-up in one of those double strollers. She was almost to the elbow of the stairwell when pop. It probably hurt like a motherfucker. There would have been palpitations, and not small ones. They'd have moved through her like waves. A series of fluid punches to the chest, shoulders, back, jaw, and gut. She would've been struggling to hold on to the stroller even before the last blinding jolt of pain galvanized her entire body. She'd have been locked up in a rigid brace for just an instant, enough time for one last thought, maybe two.

All this in front of her nineteen-month-old twins. I like to think Georgia held on to them until the last possible second. The stroller's handle becoming the single point of my sister's focus—her last totem of earthly import. When she finally let go and fell to the ground, she was most likely dead by the time she hit the floor. The twins rolled backwards down one flight of stairs before flipping upside down. My niece and nephew laid there for about an hour and a half before the mailman found them.

Miraculously giving in to my irrational demand that the hospital spend nearly a quarter of a million dollars in tests to determine the exact cause of Georgia's heart failure, and perhaps also to satisfy the curiosity of his own singular genius, Crotch discovered that the genetic defect that blew up Georgia's heart also resided in me. And it was most likely a donation from our father. Our hero. The far superior of our two parents.

Now Crotch is standing in front of me waving a piece of paper. "Thanks for signing the release, Alex." He's smiling. He has this practiced, patronizing smile.

The truth is, I *did* send him back a signed release, just not the exact same one he'd sent me. And Char and I call him "Dr. Crotch" because he buys his scrubs too small and pulls them up too high. His name is actually Park, Dr. Brian Park.

"You're welcome, Park," I say. "Glad to help. Hope you guys make the big show with it."

"Yes, but just to clarify." He's pulling something out of his fanny pack. Crotch's crew is filing in behind him. I close my eyes. I think, *Make it now. I want to go now. Zap. Bing. Pow. Now, you mutha!* I open my eyes. Still here, wearing my helmet, but now Crotch has his glasses on.

"I don't recall this verbiage in the release when my office drafted it," he says. I start to tell him there's no need to read it but it's too late.

"'N de event dat da damn patient, Alexanda' Mitchell Widerspoon, resides in an 'estended coma o' should suffa' some oda' catego'ical, debilitatin' and 'estended trauma o' neurological injury dat renders him unable t'consent t'furda' testin', surgery, o' invasive 'esaminashun'." He drops the paper very dramatically and removes his glasses.

There's nothing to say. I'm looking at him and trying to make my eyelids droop, as if I'm bored with it all. "Are you," I ask, "taking issue with my grammar?"

"Are you?" he asks in a gotcha-voice and points at me with a ringed pinky finger. Then, the mighty Park just fizzles out and drops his hand. He doesn't know what to say. My behavior is incomprehensible to a surgeon of Crotch's caliber.

He would never understand if I told him I did it because I could. I did it because it was funny at the time and because the words on the release he'd sent me had conspired to create a terrifying menu of medical macabre. I did it because asking me to put my signature at the bottom of that colossal jinx was just asking too damn much.

After I'd taken the words from the electronic form he'd sent me and bathed them in the bright blue light of capture, I dropped them into other worlds. First I translated them into Mandarin with one satisfying mouse-click. I liked the look of them and was going to print and sign, but I wanted to try them out in Latin, the language of medicine. Next I put them in Spanish, in honor of Char, and read them out loud. Feverishly, I cast them into Finnish, German, Italian, and Farsi. Finally, I discovered the Jive app, and that's where they remain because a guy appeared at my counter with a stack of old Mickey Spillane novels and interrupted me.

I like to think Georgia held on to them until the last possible second. The stroller's handle becoming the single point of my sister's focus—her last totem of earthly import.

Unable to recover from his lack of a good question, Crotch pronounces, "Dr. Witherspoon, there's no need to apologize. We know things have been difficult for you."

"No one's apologizing. And don't call me doctor."

"I shared this release"—Crotch says "release" with perfect disdain—"with Dr. Santos and . . ."

"Char! You showed this to *Char*?" This is going to be a scandal. "What the fuck? Look Park, if I blow, and it turns me into a vegetable, you can absolutely go in and retrieve your fiddle stick. But he gets to cut. Not you." I point behind Crotch to a redheaded resident whose face sprouts a constellation of red blotches. "Jones! Dr. Jones! Right? That's your name?"

"Yes," Jones says looking at Crotch. I knew this Dr. Jones once, briefly, in the fog of the past.

"Put dat in yo release and I'll sign it," I say. Crotch frowns.

Then it occurs to me. "It was you paging Char just now, wasn't it? You two set me up. She invited me to lunch today so you could ambush me in this God-forsaken hospital." Crotch puts a hand on my shoulder. I wiggle it off with a huff.

It seems Park wants to complain some more about the release, so I interrupt him and say, "Okay, already. It was a joke, Park. Remember those?" and I'm walking in the other direction. "I got to catch the el."

"No, Alex. You need to be looked at," Crotch yells after me.

For a moment I think I might just walk on. He wants to put me on a treadmill and study my long QT's. I really don't want to die on Crotch's equipment. I don't need to remind him that in 1884, in what they suspect to be the first documented case of an anchor protein mutation like mine, a teenage girl died after someone *yelled at her.*

After Crotch's inquisition, I catch the train to Arlington Heights to pick up the twins from my mother's and take them to the park to see their dad. I want to see my sister's husband get his kids back. The problem is right now Thomas doesn't really want them back. He says he's not ready. He lost his job at the *Sun-Times* a few months back. Shortly after that, the twin's day-care center alerted Social Services after he passed out in the carpool lane.

After my father died, my mother ate her way through 5,000 calories a day—cushioned in her misery by my father's considerable investments—and left Georgia and me to raise ourselves while she watched soap operas and cried on the phone to her sister. Still, Mom's the only option the twins have while Thomas is still putting whiskey in his morning coffee.

I ride the train because I don't drive anymore, which is one thing Char concedes is probably not irrational. There's no law against people with anchor protein mutations operating motor vehicles, but there should be. Char texts me to congratulate me on my checkup. This seems silly, but she's sincere. I text her back and ask her if she's in love with Crotch. It's stupid, but she'll understand. He's the Jack Nicklaus of cardiothoracics, exceptional among a field of outstanding.

The small surgical scar down my breastbone itches. It's faintly sticky and smooth, and when I scratch it, it fires back with a popping sensation. The device is a kind of internal lightning rod, and if it works the way it should, which at this point is entirely speculation, it'll counteract the repolarization of my heart and reverse the severe ventricular fibrillation. We don't know enough to predict when or even what combination of factors will trigger it, but when the big one hits (oh, and it will) the rod just may save me. It's still likely, however, that I'll hit the ground hard enough to kill myself. Hence, the helmet.

I feel like an ass carrying Crotch's little miracle inside of me. When Georgia arrested, she hit the floor so hard she cracked her skull on the radiator grate. Dark cranial blood trailed down the staircase and soaked in a pool right next to the twinks' little heads as they waited for their mother underneath the stroller.

The aftermath. Now that's the real tragedy. I think I've narrowed my problem down to this (and it's not fear of death—about that I've become somewhat groggy and trusting). It's the aftermath: my de-oxygenated blood switching off my brain, the pulling of my central power cord, the Alex-shell left to twitch and shit itself on the train platform or in line at the deli. Why do I care about the fate of the Alex-shell or about the aftermath, in general? After all, my religion is science and that ends with my vessel writhing in train-platform grime in the final throes of its remaining independent neuro-function.

I care because I know what it's like to live through the aftermath. I know all too well.

Georgia loved bugs as a little kid. She would come in from playing outside with a collection of bugs, some alive. She had long, dark curls and a chubby pink face. I'd say, "What kind of girl plays with bugs all the time?"

She'd say, "I'm not a girl. I'm a bug!"

I'd say, "You *are* a girl. You're a princess." My dad was dead, and I knew what was expected of me. I'd heard him talk like this.

Georgia would always say some nonsense back, like, "No. I'm a king. I'm a majesty."

After he died, neither of us wanted to be alone with our mom. I was happy to know Georgia was there somewhere, playing. And she'd come and find me, too, wherever I was. Georgia would come and just look at me for a second and then go away again. I knew what she wanted. It was what I wanted.

Our father died in the Denver airport. He was alone when he fell face first on the escalator, going down. I imagine him rolling out like a slapstick comic into the terminal with his houndstooth garment bag tangled up beneath him.

Once while my mother was talking in the yard with our neighbor, I interrupted them to ask if anyone at the airport had laughed at him. "You know, when he died?" I'd asked. My mother and this neighbor just stared at me. But it seemed important at the time, and it still kind of does.

Severe myocardial infarction was ruled the cause of death. That was right, *and* it was wrong. But it would be twenty-two years before we'd understand what it meant. After Georgia died, I was stoned on painkillers for a month trying to cope with our mother. I took all my vacation at once. Mom refused to get off the toilet the morning of Georgia's funeral. She actually called me in there and asked me to help her wipe her ass.

We are taught as doctors that death is part of the cycle of all living things. It's the one true inevitability of everything found in nature, and we begin the work of dying just as soon as we are born. But what's more interesting is the deluge of secret imperfections we can arrive with and the catastrophes they'll inevitably bring. All creation is in some way imperfect, genetically speaking. In theory, if this were all part of God's plan, God arranges for us down to the most invisible detail, which anyone would agree is a lot to keep up with.

And genetically speaking, our little defect is about as common as a third nostril or being born without nipples. It's duplication along a portion of an autosome. That's it. The smallest most miniscule deviation. The equivalent of an extra grain of flour in a recipe for a cake the size of a water tower.

When I get to my mom's, a Tudor decorated just the way it was the day my father died, I find the nanny's brought the twins home from pre-school and left for the day. It's two-thirty in the afternoon and Mom's on the sofa in a floral nightgown, smoking. I've told her before she shouldn't smoke in the house with the twins. I tell her this again now. We talk about the twins. Will they be tested? she wants to know. She asks about my own tests, my implant scar, my baggy jeans.

I really don't want to die on Crotch's equipment. I don't need to remind him that in 1884, in what they suspect to be the first documented case of an anchor protein mutation like mine, a teenage girl died after someone yelled at her.

She cries. She stands on swollen feet, shakes a little for effect, a kind of all-over-fat-shimmy, before waddling out to the patio.

I write her a quick note about pedal edema, hypertension, and the dangers of thrombosis and put it inside a box of Oreos that sits open on the coffee table. With that, I roll the stone back in front of this particular cave.

I find the twins holding hands on the floor of their room watching the flat-screen television my mother's bought for them.

*

Thomas is already at the park when we get there. He's wearing a sweater-vest and drinking out of a tall travel mug. He's reading the newspaper on a bench.

He takes the twins up in his arms. His eyes soften, and he brings his nose down and breathes up hard, lightly rising strands of hair off the head of the girl. He likes to read, and I help myself to the cream off the resale books for him from time to time. Today, I've got something for him in my shoulder bag.

"Thomas," I say, "I've brought you a Russian and two small children that bear a spooky resemblance to one another." The book is an early-edition Tolstoy that came to my store by way of a little old lady with a stafflike walking stick. "A good Russian will cure whatever ails you, my friend," the woman had said, pointing at my helmet.

This playground is filled with plastic rocket ships and foam planets connected by spongy expanses that are meant to resemble the surface of the moon. There's nothing to climb and nothing to swing on. Nothing here can hurt you. There's a plastic astronaut holding a sign instructing all children to remove their shoes and place them in a cubby before entering the play area. I sit on the bench next to Thomas and watch the twins logroll along the rings of Saturn.

"Your friend's office called again yesterday," Thomas says. "Dr. Park."

"And?" I'm careful not to say too much about Crotch.

"Are the twins going to die, Alex?"

I'm not sure how to answer this. The correct answer, of course, is yes.

"Of course not, Thomas. Of course not," I say.

"He thinks I should test them. He says he can bring in a crackerjack pediatric surgeon to assist with the surgery if it should come to that."

"Uh-huh," I say. "That sounds good."

"I'm thinking no," he says. "Probably no."

"Okay," I say. I'm quick to add, "Although, Park's probably the only person in the world that can help them. And he happens to be a friend of mine." This lie is as close as I want to come to persuasion.

Thomas hangs his head on this a moment, and I ignore the two tears that land on his newspaper, smearing the headline "Homecoming for Hero" into something resembling a caterpillar. "But look at you, man," he says. "How can you say that?"

"Well, at least I have a safety net of sorts in here," I say, tapping at my breastbone.

"But you walk around in a blue epilepsy helmet. You've lost your job," he says.

"I quit my job. They're down on helmets at that hospital. Even in podiatry," I say, and he frowns at me in profile. And there it is: the aftermath. The utter defeat of Thomas who used to tell the best jokes and bought my sister the townhouse she'd wanted instead of deflating her with the tiresome but practical truth, which was that they couldn't afford it.

All of a sudden, a wave hits me in the chest. It's like a thick, heavy fish turning over inside my ribcage. I jump off the bench without a word and make for the nearest plastic rocket ship. I slip on a divot in the moon's surface and go down hard. *Not in front of the twinks. Not in front of Thomas.* I scramble to a blue spaceship and crab-crawl through its tiny entrance as quickly as I allow myself. I'm sitting in the black of its hollow. I'm sucking in the heavy chalk-scent of playground dust and dirty socks. *Let it be quick*—this is the thought behind which I concentrate what I assume to be my fleeting, and I fear wholly inadequate, human will—like blowing a fuse. *Just flip my fucking switch already.*

One more flop of the fish. I bring my head down between my knees and let my helmet rest there. At this moment—perhaps the moment nearest death, or the latest miracle in cardiothoracic science, or maybe even the peak of a monstrous anxiety attack—I'm seeing myself from all sides. Here, in this recycled tire and soda can universe, I've finally come into focus. I've fallen face forward into a little heap, and I immediately understand that I'm helmeted yet unprepared. How could I be? Have I ever been? What person hurling forward on this rock of bumbling happenchance has any right to feel prepared?

Suddenly, the twins speak in unison, "What you doing, Uncle Alex?"

I open my eyes and see two pair of identical shoes in my eye-line. I lift my head from the ground and wipe off some playground debris that's affixed to my chin. I poke into the tender divots it's left behind.

If it must, the body will eventually conquer by submission. Sure, initially there's discomfort, then pain, then inflammation, and eventually infection. Yet if all else fails, a healthy human body will ultimately surrender and accommodate. If I'd lain here three months, my skin would've swallowed this debris: mulch, pebble, and matchstick. It would've snaked right over it.

"Can I wear your helmet?" the boy asks.

"Another day, buddy," I say.

I make my way out of the ship and back to the bench where their father is sitting. Thomas is just as I left him. "You should do it," I say. "Call Park. I think you need to know. Whatever it is." Then I hesitate before adding, "I'll help you."

"And what about you?" he asks. Thomas is squinting into the sun behind me.

*

I've been slowly packing some of the stuff in our apartment. Char and I fought like crazy about it when she first caught me, but then she decided to let it go. I don't want her to have to pack up my stuff someday. I imagine her rummaging through my old yearbooks, pictures of my ex-girlfriends, my porn.

I'm on a stepladder in the closet jostling the contents of a box. I pull it down and open the lid. On top, there's a picture of my dad teaching Georgia and me to swing a plastic golf club. She has that look of determination on her chubby little face. I'm hovering behind her, patronizing, interested. I hold the photo close to my chest. It hurts. When they taught us about death in medical school like they knew something, I suspect even they knew they were wrong.

"Alex." She startles me. Char's standing in the doorway of our bedroom with her coat on. "Will you please stop packing this place up, baby?" She sits on the edge of the bed. "Come down. Sit by me."

I do.

"I'm glad to see that you're standing on the stool without your helmet. For you, this is bravery," she says. I'm sure she doesn't mean this as an insult. Her face is relaxed. She asks about the twins, my mother, then "Are you hungry?"

"I thought you were paged for surgery," I say sarcastically. "That was fast." She knows I've figured out that the page she got back at the hospital was just a signal from Crotch.

"I used to find you so intimidating, Alex," she says. I tense up at her tone, although she's trying to keep it even. "I grew up with four brothers and they made me strong. I came to medical school and everyone was so white and rich. And scared. These people with money, so scared. But you were confident. And handsome." She's saying this and sitting like a visitor would sit on a bed. She's still wearing her coat. "Where's that man gone? And don't say your heart. All that's changed is a diagnosis. That's it. Every one of us has rogue cells, latent diseases, genetic anomalies. I could slip and die in the shower tomorrow, Alex."

I'm too cowardly to tell her that I want to spare her the aftermath and that I've become too afraid for this life. I could say, I'm sick of your fucking tenacity. I almost say, All I want is a playmate. "These things take time," I say.

"Alex, you sound like your mother."

"I find you intimidating now, Char." I say. "And it's not a turn-on anymore. I think if you could just back off a bit . . . ." I instinctively reach for my helmet on the nightstand then rethink it.

"Would you prefer for me to stop fighting?" Char asks. "Are you asking me to give up on you?"

"If you must, you must," I say. But really, I want to fall into her lap. I want to cry hard, just this once, and then wipe my face with her hair. But I know this sort of thing just can't be done with this sort of woman.

"If I must?" she asks. She looks disgusted. She stands to leave. "Who's going to tell you the truth, Alex? You need the *truth*." This next part comes out uncharacteristically squeaky, "Not your mother! Not poor, pathetic Thomas." She takes a breath and steadies her eyes on me before directing a slow lateral gaze toward my helmet. "Put it back on," she says. "I can't do this anymore. I'm leaving."

And she did.

But she came back. Char came right back but she'd just missed me.

A NOTE REGARDING THE AFTERMATH

Fear and love are nonlinear systems. Instead, they follow the chaos model. But even systems that appear chaotic—like cancer, or swarms, or people—given simple rules will eventually settle into a limited, stable pattern. Simplicity always triumphs, even on the grandest scale. The aftermath is really just this: fear. And for this reason, Charla Santos is going to be just fine.

As for death, well I admit that came as a surprise. In the end, it was something with which I was already quite familiar. So when they tell you about death, don't believe them. It's nothing like that. It's infinitely simpler than that. Infinitely simple, yet incomprehensibly expansive. It is both.

Your Friend,
Casco

Melanie Braverman
The World with Us in It
(excerpt)

Every few days we find another bird dead in the wrack, neck broken in the waves, an eider's breast flashing white in the glare, a gull's spanned wing arrayed to show how majestic it really is. Was. Wind! Molly said, "If I could punch the wind, I would." I dream of people I used to know and walk my dog when I get up. Leaving the house is like pushing against will. The part of our beach with no building on it receives the brunt of the tide's wash, as if the petulance of the human world cannot bear to let it sit empty: tires, bottles, timber, sails, fishnets, buoys, shoes. That spot drives my poor dog wild as the men who sleep their drunks off curled in overturned dinghies beneath the town pier. The pier itself will not stand in such a wind.

"Everyone thinks your father looks great now because he's thin, but he doesn't," my mother reports to me over the phone, "he looks old and gray and sick." She sat behind him at a recital, my father's wife next to him, smart cap of silver hair like a well-fed chickadee on the bough. My younger brother's children plunked their nervous tunes, the girl methodical, the boy in a rush. When I talk to my father he says, "How's your mother doing *really*," sure that something important is being withheld, the way it's always been, as if we alone had drawn that aged circle in the sand. I tell him everything but this: there's a dark spot on one of her lungs, small but dense as a moon. Who will we be when she goes.

Snow shows itself in the halo of the yellow streetlight I looked at every night as a child, illuminating the same patch of street that must be worn a little thinner now from so many years of shine. Big houses on the street are for sale, looking for young families to fill their rooms as ours did forty years ago. My mother's house is stalwart, smack in the center of three streets that lead into the neighborhood where all the traffic ends up. I'm surprised, but she keeps it cool enough even for me to be comfortable with my growing intolerance of heat. But look: my mother has begun to waver; around her face her outline is a little smudged, a soft pencil has drawn her in. It won't last, it's a ripple on my mother's pond. She says she's aged but it's the poison on march in her raging veins calling her cells back into ranks like a general woken by her flapping tent, war unceasing despite her need or desire to sleep.

Stephen Burt
Felinity

AFTER BAUDELAIRE

The indifferent, the out of love, people so bored with their work
that they can't stop talking about it, the revved-up teens
unwilling to gaze out the window—none would spare

a minute for the diffident, dark-
eared, wide-eyed cat blinking up out of sleep as she cleans
one more foreclaw, then hides her head in our chair,

tongue slightly out, as usual: more rude
to human beings than any human being
should be. She wants to get spanked.

Her brothers dash off but go limp if you catch them fleeing,
then track us down after half-hearted attempts to hide
or settle on us as we sleep; that's how they keep warm.

They see that we see that they do not wish to be thanked.
They hiss every morning . . . so easy to know what they need
and set it before them, and know we have done them no harm.

There

Like waking from something, but not from a dream

      so sleepy
there was really nothing there.
I had to pull over right away,
get off the road.

In Lebanon, New Hampshire,
which is not an example,
a bridge with an upward curve like a lowercase n
rises above the terrestrial
road surface, beautiful guardrails, beautiful sun

      hills
like rehearsal curtains,
thick and heavy, a uniform green.
There's a ten-speed bike on a gingerbread porch,
its handbrakes askew like the talons of bats,

              an Infant of Prague House.
The wooden sign says only *Rooms.*

The sky is a word. The sky is a womb. The sky
befits a summer afternoon
with somewhere else I ought to be,
but not yet.

Two girls in oversized running shoes find
each other and, looking sullen together,
disappear over the rise,

while pale strips of cloud soothe the *Nouveauté
Boutique*, Hisick's Clothing and Uniforms
(on show: a firefighter's uniform)
and the Back-to-School Sale conducted
from a tent in rescue orange,

across the street from the LISTEN thrift store.
The rest of the clouds just go, passing lightly, carefully
over the town and my life as well, telling
it gently, *There now*, or just *There*.

Nathan Huffstutter
After I Smothered the Baby

It's funny how a thing'll just pop into your head. I hadn't even got back in my mind yet, still splashing cold water, backside my neck, forearms, good God, the disaster my hair, and straight out the blue, boppity-boo, I got to thinkin' about Evie's smoke alarm story. Which is kinda funny, you know, 'cause that's a funny story.

Before then, I don't know how long I had the faucet runnin'—when I sunk my hands in the basin, the water'd puddle up and pool onto the counter, but I kept right on doin' it. My skin's still all pin-prickly and swole, and that cold water felt good. Standing there, clear as day, I thought of Evie's story—only, not the way she usually tells it. She likes to make sure she got your attention, so she starts off in one of those whisper-voices, saying about the cold, dark house, dead of night, dead of winter. This time, though, I wasn't thinking about it like a story I'd heard, it was more like I was right there watching it happen, just without actually being there, without actually being a part. This was quick soon after the boys got deployed, and Evie had her momma staying over most nights. Only this night, this night her momma wasn't there and Evie was alone with Shayanne. Dark as dark, colder than a you-know-what, they're both fast asleep and it's like I'm a shadow, creepin' down Evie's hallway . . . .

WHEEEE-YOOO! WHEEEE-YOOO!

Pow—Evie's a missile. Lights out the bedroom, don't touch down 'til she gets to the crib. Grabs Shayanne, lickity-split, they're out safe in the driveway. Shay, she's too shocked to cry or nothin', and Evie's backing further out onto the sidewalk. She can see her breath, dead quiet, all the neighbors, no lights—even that crazy alarm's stopped. No sign of smoke. Not from the windows, or under the door, but Shay, she's still more or less a baby, Evie can't just plop her down and peek back inside. So they both stand out there, feels about forever, watching their breath, 'til finally Evie goes *this is effing ridiculous*. Her arms've gone tingly and numb from holding Shayanne, no kind of nothin' to lean on, so finally she carries her in, going from room to room. Bedrooms, bathroom, closets, laundry: no smoke, no fire. So she puts Shay in her crib, worries for a whole 'nother forever, then finally goes back to bed.

WHEEEE-YOOO! WHEEEE-YOOO!

I hear the noise and see like I'm bending down right over Shay's crib. And instead of coming in runnin', this time Evie's more like walkin' fast—by the time she turns the corner, Shay's already shakin' the bars and screamin' bloody murder. Evie picks Shayanne out, but insteada rushin' for the front door, first she starts checking around: bedrooms, bathroom, and before she even gets to the closets, the alarm up and quits. No smoke. No fire. So she rocks Shay back to sleep, then goes and takes one of the dining chairs out into the hall. Right at this part, when she's the one tellin' it, this is where Evie starts gettin' her first little laughs—she actually swears the dirty words under her breath, sonofa-this, mother-that, piece-of-you-know-what, the whole time pretending she's rifling through the toy chest, lookin' for a talkin' bear or a choo-choo or anythin' what got a workin' battery. Only it don't seem so funny when I'm watching right close, I can hear the snap in all them curse words, and as she pops each little battery hatch, I can see how angry her hands is shakin'. Evie ain't laughin' either, not when she gets up on that dining chair, not when she changes a good battery into the alarm, and she ain't laughin' when she slams the chair back at the table and drags on down to bed.

WHEEEE-YOOO! WHEEEE-YOOO!

I'd snapped out of it enough to stop the water runnin', but to be honest, I couldn't say how long I kept standin' at the mirror, watchin' my looks. It wasn't that I didn't recognize myself, I just couldn't recognize how I come to be so far gone. The water was circlin' the drain, suckin' on down, but all I could hear was that shrieking alarm. That, and I could hear Shayanne cryin', only this time, this time her cry ain't scared, it's just plain mad. Evie, too. In the mirror, I could see Evie blaze out into the hallway, fourteen different kinds of pissed off. When we got a group of us girls together, right here's where Evie's up on her feet, wavin' her arms like a crazy person, and all us girls, we're 'bout to die laughin', just how Evie acts it all out: climbing up on that dining chair, pulling out the fresh battery, yanking wires, damn near tearing the whole thing out the ceiling.

And just like that, the noise stops.

I don't hear nothin' either, standin' there at the mirror, Lord, what a sight, and over my shoulder, instead of rockin' Shayanne back to sleep, I watch Evie carry her into the big bed, tucking her under the covers and rubbing her little back until they both drift off.

WHEEEE-YOOO! WHEEEE-YOOO!

To be honest, I couldn't say how long I kept standin' at the mirror, watchin' my looks. It wasn't that I didn't recognize myself, I just couldn't recognize how I come to be so far gone.

One time, a couple us girls, we's laughin' so hard we got tears, but right here they started addin' in, sayin' no matter how tired you get, you ain't never too tired to pick up your little ones. The way they was talkin', it come off kinda huggy and sweet, sayin' how no matter what, you always got that last strength left. And I just nodded, it made perfect sense at the time—reachin' for your babies, it ain't like movin' your neighbors, where when you hit the wall, ain't no way you can lift one more lousy box.

Now, seein' Evie do all that rockin' and back-rubbin', all those times lugging Shayanne this way and that, I know it's all she can do to pull herself sitting up. And even with that alarm wailing away, Shay, she's so exhausted she barely whimpers, just grinding her little face deeper and deeper into the pillow. The actual mattress, Evie's got that high up on a box spring and rails, so she can't just leave Shay lying there—when she picks her off the bed, ain't nothing huggy or sweet about it, just a face that's all pain. Right then, I understood—there ain't no deep-down, hidden kind of strength. When you given all you got to give, if you got to give even more, it takes ripping and tearing from your own insides. And if you're just loadin' your neighbors' U-Haul, well, you got sense enough to know those boxes ain't worth it.

So Evie, she plops Shayanne on the hall carpet, then goes back on through, bedrooms, bathroom, closets—bingo. They hadn't been here in family housing that long, and Evie'd never noticed the fire detector up above the laundry. One more time, she fetches that dining chair, gets up, yanks the battery, the plastic cover, a whole cloud of plaster, she's jerking and twisting all the wires, and just like that, the noise stops.

It's quiet.

Only now it's closer to early than late, so Evie puts Shay in front the cartoons, starts the coffee pot, and goes and gets the Yellow Pages. Look out—she's fixing to lay into someone, and good. Except the government listings don't really have noplace right to call, so she jimmies Devlin's file drawer, starts shufflin' through his enlistment papers, tryin' to find a number for the housing department.

WHEEEE-YOOO! WHEEEE-YOOO!

The look Evie gets, no matter how many times you heard the story, it's priceless. She does like she's stabbing a butcher knife, same as a psycho in the movies, and all us girls, we'll be laughin', clappin', goin' "Stop, stop, stop," 'cause we could picture feelin' the exact same.

That wailing, though, they ain't really got no idea. Not when it comes constant. Then all that noise surrounds, chokin' on down, 'til the walls, the ceiling, feels like everything's cracking up and caving in. Evie's walking with her head ducked, them two alarms, howling so fierce she gotta keep herself leaned forward, hoping the sound'll only hit off her back and shoulders. The two plastic housings, the ones she tore off the walls, those don't make no noise—it's a couple metal ringers, deep in the drywall. When she sees that, Evie gets this strange sort of calm. Ain't nothing left to do, she sits herself right in the middle of the floor, crosslegged, squeezing her baby tight to her chest. She just holds on—either the noise'll stop, or it'll bury them both alive.

Lucky thing. It stops.

There's a number, Evie wrote it from Devlin's drawer, but she don't call right away—everything in these units gotta be up to code, typical military, so real careful, still calm, she gets the dining chair, plugs in all the batteries and wires, then screws everything back to the walls. She's too tired to talk the whole thing through, so she figures she'll just wait 'til the alarms go again—that ways, she won't have to explain, she can just dial the number and hold up the phone.

So she waits. And waits. And waits.

And that's the ending joke—to this day, Evie don't know what set off those alarms. Or, what made 'em stop for good.

It's still quiet.

Lookin' out, out here in the dark and mist, ain't much to see either—everyone else got their lights off, blinds down. This here front doorstep, the cool concrete, I always liked this spot. Before setting down, first I had to brush aside a pile of newspapers. Sorta said it all, same as the feeling coming down the hallway. Tiptoeing, still that carved-out pain from the stitches where I ripped, and those quiet steps felt like coming home from being gone. Gone long enough that silence settles over everything, so you come in whisperin', making sure you don't kick nothin' up or disturb it too sudden.

The whole house was dark, all but the message machine, flashing eight, nine, ten.

Most of those, I can already guess—when it comes daylight, I got to be callin' Evie. She stopped over yesterday, or coulda been the day before. No start, no finish, near about impossible to keep one day separate from the next. Either way, it wasn't so long ago, we was inside at the sofa and she kept sucking her lip, squintin', trying not to cry. Then, she did. She started rubbing between my shoulders, sayin' I was this amazing person, tellin' what a great job I was doin'. Only, even then I could tell it wasn't real compliments, just how you talk nice at someone flat on their face. I don't think I said nothing back, and I'm not sure if my looks showed how empty I felt—probably, 'cause Evie got to cryin' harder. Before leavin', she promised she was gonna convince my momma she had to come fly back out, no matter if she could get the time from work or not.

I don't know if Evie ever got ahold of her—maybe that's what's in the messages.

Not that it matters now. This dark, so much out there you don't need to see, and first it kept all that covered, lettin' me focus in close. The mist, too—it isn't the soaking kind, more floaty and soft, and for a few minutes, here in this night air, seemed everything was finally back in front of me, my whole life was still possible. Before too long, though, my eyes got to adjust and I started seeing more regular. Then, all that tired set back in, two heavy bootheels, one on each shoulder. That weight, can't imagine lasting 'til daybreak, and even if I do, no way I'll be able to talk through the whole thing. But that's all right. I can call Evie, and all I'll have to do is hold up the phone. When she hears this quiet, this still, I won't have to explain. She'll hear it, and she'll know.

Laura Kasischke
Beautiful Classmate
from the Past

She sat in front of me in
math, as I
coughed and scratched, had
menstrual pain and
Mr. Nestor could never
remember my name.

The laziness
of her hair, all
opium and amazing
that she too has grown
older as we've aged.
Not even dead.
The elevator

gliding silently between
the floors of a tower all
night for thirty
years. No one

inside, but
something riding
along for the ride, never

asking itself why.

Like this
preserved girl all
laid out for the exhibit
along with certain
items
they found with her:

A scrap of cloth,
four beads, the skull
of a bird she'd eaten.

Midnight

At midnight the conductor grinds the whole thing to a halt. All

the days in their separate cars crammed with the elementary particles
that would have made the hours possible until dawn, and

then the slow
risings and the washings,

and then the hurried
breakfasts, the many
lunches wrapped in silver foil, the old complaints, *We're
out of paper towels. Where are my keys? We're going to be late.*

The traffic jams.
The weekend plans.

But now the conductor's stepped onto the tracks, and sauntered off.
The haunted playground. The oncologist. The postman. The woman
who agreed to do my taxes. Her daughter, who
laundered my winter jacket. I
call and call

out to them all
and they don't answer.

Her conductor has walked off
I hear someone say.

He is not in the train.
He is not in the station.

Look, I brought you this far
He breathes into my hair:

The middle of the night.
The middle of nowhere.

Room

There's a room inside myself
I've never seen.
There's

a bed there, and
on a nightstand, photographs
in frames. But

whose faces?

A violet
vase on a vanity: I've

held it in my hands. *Tearful
apology.* And

under my bed
in narrow boxes?
And if I open the desk
drawer, or
the dresser?

Well, just
the usual soft
folded things.
Silky
rectangles.
Knitted
squares.
A glove.
A stocking.
A loss, eternally.
And a window

(I'm sure of this)
which looks out onto green
pasture.
An apple tree.

And, beneath the tree, my
grandmother
in a housedress
in a lounge chair, sipping
a cool drink, not

even wondering
where she went or, where,
all these years,
she's been.

Adam Felts
Sam

The last time I saw Sam he was dead in the middle of his living room. His white tee shirt was soaked from the bottle of vodka he had spilled over his chest. He was surrounded by pills that never made it into him, so many pills and their bottles, as if they were ants and he was their queen and they were gathered around him for a kind of wake or funeral. He was curled up into a ball as though he was trying to climb into himself, to escape from something awful and great and terrible and everywhere.

I stood in front of him and we were both motionless because he was dead and I was seeing him dead and I needed to say or break something or yell or run but instead I just stood there. I couldn't look at him—only glance, he being a dense sun of shock and incomprehensibility.

It was like one of those dreams where you have to tell somebody something but you can't. You're standing right in front of them and they're listening but the words don't form and you're just opening and closing your mouth like a fish or someone pretending to be a fish. I've had that dream a lot.

Until he died, Sam was my best friend. Until he died, I thought Sam and I knew everything about each other. We went to school together, chose not to keep going to school together, found and rented tiny houses in a broken-down neighborhood together and scored low-paying jobs together and got drunk and stumbled to McDonald's in the middle of the night on the weekends together. All the way from fuzzy intangible childhood till when we were dysfunctional dead-end young adults I thought I knew everything about Sam, until he died.

*

I should have known something was wrong with Sam after that night he told me to hit him. It was strange because he wasn't drunk. I was. We were at his place, in his living room, the same room where he killed himself a few months later.

"Are we in *Fight Club*, now?" I asked him.

"No," he said. "That movie sucked. Come on, punch me." We were both standing.

"Punch you where?"

"In the face."

"Why?"

"I don't know. Just hit me here in the face." He pointed to it as if he thought I needed directions.

"Are you really not going to hit me? I'm letting you punch me," he said. "In the face. How many times have you punched someone in the face?"

"Never."

"Well." He leaned forward, his face jutting out, a welcoming target.

He was just hanging there in front of me, not even braced for it. He was asking for it. Literally.

"I can't do it."

"Why not?"

"It just seems like a bad idea, intrinsically speaking. I don't think I would have much to gain from it, you know?"

He hit me in the chest, a weak little jab near my heart, and gave me an imploring look. "I just hit you," he said. "You've gotta hit me back." He hit me again, harder.

"Fuck off," I said, laughing. I pushed him away. He had one of those excellent grins, one of those something-has-to-happen faces. He pushed me back.

"Come on!" he said. "We're fighting. You have to hit me in the face!" He hit me again in the chest, still harder.

"If you hit me again I'm going to hold you down and make you eat beetles," I said, stumbling over a couple words.

"That's not at all what I'm asking you to do!" he said. "Hit me!" He hit me again, same place, even harder. Blood red flashed in front of my eyes, fight-or-flight, animal instincts telling me to go for weak points and soft spots.

"Dude, seriously, fucking quit," I said.

"You haven't hit me yet," he said. "We're fighting. You gotta hit me." And he punched me in that same spot and I swung back, right at his jaw, and connected.

I heard Sam's head hit the floor as I clutched my fist in blinding black pain. My smallest two knuckles were bleeding, the skin ripped off. I sucked the blood off of them while I squeezed my damaged hand with the other to try to force out the hurt.

Sam was lying on the ground, clutching his head, laughing. I probably should have been concerned by this, but it wasn't a crazy laugh. It seemed perfectly unremarkable to me, at that moment. He laughed like someone who unexpectedly gets kissed by a decent-looking girl, or someone who finds a soaked twenty dollar bill in a gutter on a rainy night. Then he spat out a hunk of blood. It was a surprisingly good punch. He got slowly up to his feet, his mouth open, his tongue flitting about, surveying the damage.

"You knocked out my tooth, dude." He laughed, again. "You knocked out my fucking tooth." He slapped me on the shoulder and walked past me into the bathroom. I stood there in something of a pained daze, my right hand swelling up before my eyes, sobered by a combination of pain and surreality.

I followed him into the bathroom. He was at the sink, slurping water out of his cupped hands and spitting it back out faint red. I stood behind him awkwardly, still squeezing my hand, watching him tend his wounds. I noticed that he had a lot of razors on the rim of the sink, maybe seven straight razors all neatly arranged around the basin.

"What's with all the cutlery?" I asked. Suddenly he switched the sink off.

"Oh," he said. "I'm a hairy, hairy man, my friend, if I don't keep up with myself. I try to keep an arsenal of shaveware ready at all times." He carefully picked all the razors off the sink with two fingers, like a crane. He deposited them in his medicine cabinet and led me out of the bathroom.

He turned around smiling as widely as he could to show off the new hole in his grin. It gave a nice authenticity to him, a homeless person aesthetic.

"Check it the fuck out," he said, pointing to the newfound gap in the upper-left corner of his mouth. "I'm a war veteran."

I held up my ruined hand to his face. "I think I might have PTSD," I said.

He said, "We both just lost our face-punching virginity. Was it as good for you as it was for me?"

Sam had a girlfriend, or a girl, or a person he had sex with and talked to, probably. Because I hung out with Sam I inevitably hung out with her, and during that time I managed to develop a great and healthy dislike for every fiber of her being. She was a tiny little girl with breasts too big for her body and one of those mean little faces with hard little eyes smothered in makeup to hide how cold and shallow they were.

She was attractive in the way that a porn star or a cheeseburger is attractive, that way where whenever you eye her you get an inescapable feeling of guilt afterward.

I wasn't sure if they even really liked each other. They never fought; I always thought that one day Sam would just explode like he did and that would be the end of everything, he'd tar and feather her or something, but no. Sam got quiet around her, for some reason, like something in him just turned off. It bothered me.

I dealt with it by fighting Sam's girlfriend. I'd call her a bitch and throw half-full beer cans at her and she'd chase me around swinging at me with a pool cue while I ran away

Fuck off, I said, laughing. I pushed him away. He had one of those excellent grins, one of those something-has-to-happen faces.

screaming and Sam would sit on the couch and laugh and laugh and laugh. He'd always cheer her on, tell her to aim for the forehead for maximum damage. I think deep down, really, we all enjoyed it.

After I punched Sam, she called me at work. I was employed at Walgreen's, which sounds bad, but I had powered my way in a few years to become assistant manager. I made a pretty comfortable living. Sometimes Sam would come in during his lunch break at McDonald's and steal a pack of Robitussin capsules. Getting drunk at work is pathetic, he explained, but being stoned off your ass at work on Robitussin is hilarious. Being assistant manager meant that I could cover for Sam if he ever got caught, which he never did; it also meant that I could take phone calls from his girlfriend at my leisure, which I never did, except for once.

"Hello?" I had given her my number as a formality. I didn't actually expect her to call it.

"Why did you punch Sam in the face?"

"He asked me to do it," I said.

"You don't do the things he tells you to do," she said, as though she were talking to a child. I did not like her.

"I was drunk. I'll be more careful next time, alright?"

"You need to take care of him. Do you understand? You're his best friend and—"

"Sam doesn't *need* anyone to take care of him," I interrupted.

"Could you please shut up for a second?" she said. "You have to look out for him. You should know that already. You need to take care of him."

"You really just don't know him, do you?" I said.

"What?"

"Sam is who he is. He's always been that way for as long as I can remember and he's always been alright. Just because you don't get that doesn't mean you can call me and bitch me out at work."

"You cannot be serious," she said.

"I am completely serious."

"You don't get it," she said. There was something in her voice that I had never heard before. "You really really don't. Just don't hit him again, okay?"

There was only one other time that we spoke on the phone. In the middle of his apartment with him dead in front of me, I called Sam's girlfriend.

The phone rang once, twice, three times. I knew she was awake because she had to be at a time like this, and she was. She picked up on the sixth ring.

"Hello?"

"Hello?" I said.

"Hello?" she said again.

"Sam's dead," I said. "Sam's dead in front of me."

"What?" she said, and that sent me into a fit of rage; she sent me into a fit of rage because I could tell by her voice that she believed immediately that this idea, this crazed, insane, impossible notion that Sam was dead, was real.

"What the fuck happened?" I said. "What is this? What happened? What the fuck is this?" And already she was crying, sobbing, useless.

"What the fuck?" I screamed, phone pressed against my face, and I fell to my knees, put my head to the floor, recoiled in horror and rolled pathetically backward when I realized that I was only a couple feet away from the dead Sam. "What the fuck is this?" For some awful reason she was still on the phone with me sobbing pathetically, jarringly, but she was all that was left for me to scream at because I was afraid to go close enough to Sam's dead face so that he might hear me.

"Fuck you," I cried finally, my head pressed into the crook of my arm, the other arm pressing my phone against my face as hard as it could. "Fuck you and this, fuck you, fuck you."

But by the first fuck you, I supposed, she had hung up, and I was left alone with Sam and his empty bottle and those little pills that never made it into him.

*

I had the problems you'd expect after finding one's best friend dead in the middle of his living room. I had dreams about him being there and dreams about him not being there, and either way I'd wake up shaking uncontrollably. Certain smells—Sam smells—would send me into paroxysms of crippling pain. Vodka was one of them. I could never drink vodka again.

But those things weren't the problem. Sam was dead and I didn't know why. It kept me up at night, piecing together certain things that he'd said and did, trying to find a narrative that ended with him dead in the middle of a room smelling of alcohol, bile, emptied bowels, and body odor, but that narrative just didn't exist.

Sam did crazy things. It was always like that: Everything would be quiet and suddenly Sam would just heat up, demand that we do something, anything, suggest dressing up in all black and breaking into a museum and hurling buckets of urine onto the most expensive paintings. We never got around to doing that.

Suburbia and Sam were a perfect match. We were confined to a sprawl of lily-white houses and lawns trimmed pristine by bored retirees, commanded by middle-aged couples gingerly walking strollers and Labradors that left giant shits in the streets. You could do anything you wanted as long as you could run fast enough to get away with it. Sam tore road signs out of the ground, blocked off streets with traffic cones, stole lawn gnomes and punted them over houses, broke into peoples' front doors just so that he could run out the back. And I was there with him, for most of it.

We had routes. The most important route was the McDonald's route, a stretch of suburban road lined with dark and perpetually dead woods whose skeletal branches hung down over the pavement far enough that you'd have to duck to avoid getting your eyes stabbed out. It had the distinction of leading to McDonald's as well as being littered with a few dead houses and a grimy Italian pizza place or two. You didn't fuck with the Italians—they were the only real ethnic group that our town held claim to. They were a temperamental bunch with severe entitlement issues.

Sam fucked with the Italians. The pizza place on the McDonald's route,—Luigi's, Jesus Christ—was a prime target for us.

Out in front of Luigi's they had a sign with those cheap rearrangeable letters that advertised whatever special they were selling that day or week or whatever. One day I was tired of Sam having all the bright ideas. The sign spelled out the words *tasty, parmesan, sausage,* among others. It offered me the freedom necessary to have an outburst of creative energy.

I walked up to the sign and started pulling letters off. "What the fuck're you doing?" Sam asked.

Pussy—I had rearranged five of the letters I had torn off—displayed proudly as the establishment's leading dish. I stepped back to survey my fine work.

"Oh," Sam said. "Oh. Pussy!" he finally said. "That's pretty good! Well played!"

It was early evening with the sun barely considering leaving, but there were no cars out. We kept on down the McDonald's route quietly, hands in our pockets.

"Pussy," Sam said. "You're a fucking dumbass."

"You said earlier that it was well played," I retorted.

"I've changed my mind. You could have done something so much better. Skullfuck. That would have been hilarious."

"They didn't have enough letters for Skullfuck. Do they even have the letter K in Italy?"

"I have no idea. Wait. Hold up." He stopped and turned around. There was a car coming up from behind us, fast, its headlights turned up to max. "It's the Italians," Sam said. "It's the fucking Italians. Run. Run!" He grabbed me by the arm and pulled me along with him. I was staring at the oncoming car in disbelief as it sped toward us, came up alongside us, slowed, stopped, opened its doors.

We ran. Sam didn't look back. I did. We really were being chased, surreally, insanely, the silhouettes of two men in step behind us as we stumbled away in crimson swirling terror. Sam still had his hand around my wrist. Suddenly he wrenched me off the road toward the dense and inconsiderate woods. There was no way we'd be able to get through them, no way. We would get stuck.

But when we burst through the initial skeletal wall of branches we landed upon a trail. Like an unholy guide leading me through uncharted hell, Sam pulled me down it.

The Italians had followed us. I could hear them crashing through that shield of branches, the soft din of their footsteps striking the hardened dirt. I had stopped looking back. Sam had become my savior. I looked only at where he was going.

The trail led us into a larger clearing and then Sam stopped. We had reached the end of the line.

They entered the clearing. The first one was an absolute dwarf, four-foot-ten, decked out in an all-black sweatsuit, covered in perspiration and gasping for breath. The second one must've been twice as tall as the first, stood a ways behind him silently, his arms crossed in a black sleeveless shirt, a gold chain hanging down to the middle of his chest.

The first one was clearly the brains. "Letters," he panted. "Fucking letters."

The second just stood there with a dazed yet purposeful look on his face and the strongest aura of stupidity I had ever felt coming from a human being. I figured that if we tried to run past him he would simply grab us in each hand and smash our heads together repeatedly.

"What'd you do with the fucking letters," the first one finally said. Sam and I stood there in utter disbelief, terror, shame, silence. I was the one who had done it. It was up to me to explain.

"Listen," the Italian said. "It's not easy running a fucking business. We barely break even as it is. I can't afford any new fucking letters. What did you do with the fucking letters?"

Silence.

"What the hell is this shit, taking

I'd call her a bitch and throw half-full beer cans at her and she'd chase me around swinging at me with a pool cue while I ran away screaming and Sam would sit on the couch and laugh and laugh and laugh.

peoples' letters. I'm a working man, trying to make a living, and kids like you come around and just go and take my letters and I'm near fucking broke and you kids think letters just grow off fucking trees . . . ."

"We rearranged them," Sam said suddenly. I craned my head to look at him, still paralyzed with terror. His face was lit up, his eyes sparkling. "We just rearranged them. We didn't take your letters. We made your sign say *Pussy*. Get it? Pussy! Your special is Pussy!"

"Oh," the Italian said. "Well then," and he started laughing, and Sam started laughing, and I started laughing, and the second Italian started laughing, after a reasonable delay. "You should've made the sign say Tits, then!" He laughed. "Tits!"

And Sam laughed. "Tits," he said. "That's great," he said.

"That's some good shit," the Italian said. "Listen," he said. "You guys come down to my restaurant anytime, I'll give you a free slice. You guys just come right on in and I'll hook you up, alright?"

"Okay," Sam said.

"Let's get the fuck out of here," the first Italian said. "Today's special: Tits!" he laughed, as they disappeared. We could hear their car peel off into the evening as we stood there still panting for breath.

Finally I asked Sam, "How did you do that?"

"Do what?"

"How did you find this trail? No one goes in these woods."

"Oh," Sam said. "I don't know."

"Have you been here before?"

"Of course not. This place is a shithole."

"This has got to be the only clearing in these whole woods, though."

"Yeah," Sam said. "Divine intervention, I guess."

Once Sam was so drunk on the way to McDonald's that we had to hold hands for him to stay upright. His grip ripped the skin off of the thumb that I would later use to punch him in the face. It left a scar that looks like Connecticut.

I took a lot of lone walks down the McDonald's route after Sam died, walking and thinking and walking and thinking and walking. I stopped before I reached the McDonald's because McDonald's had become one of those smells that caused pain.

I would walk and think about Sam and try to get that last piece of the narrative.

I imagined him with his head in his girlfriend's lap. He would have sobbed while she scratched his head and softly consoled him. I imagined him writing poetry in an unlit room about deadness. I imagined him taking pills to defeat some impossible, all-encompassing pain and then being in too much pain and then taking too many pills and then dying on the floor of his living room.

Sam wouldn't do any of those things. He just wouldn't.

So like a conspiracy theorist hiding in soiled white underwear in his mother's basement I tried to create a narrative about something that I did not understand.

Sam drank a lot. Alcoholic Sam would make sense. But then again drinking for him was more an extreme sport than a habit. He'd plug his nose, flip a bottle upside down well above his upturned face and let the booze drain into his mouth like a waterfall. He taped wine bottles to his hands and broke them against trees when he had to piss.

Sam didn't have enough self-control to be an alcoholic. His death would have been a lot more climactic if it were that. A lot more interesting.

That was just it. Sam died wrong. Sam would have crashed an SUV into an orphanage or eaten marshmallows until he died of asphyxiation or wrestled a bear and thrown the match out of respect. Sam died like a person who wasn't Sam.

He had a funeral. His parents were there and my parents were there and his girlfriend was there. There was no speaking between any of us. It started at a chapel.

God was involved. A preacher spoke and I tried to listen to him in hopes that maybe he would have some otherworldly answer to my tortured questions but I quickly lost interest. I found myself staring at the back of Sam's girlfriend's head while the preacher spoke. Her hair had streaks of blonde in it. I hadn't spoken to her since the night I found him dead.

I went up and looked at him in the coffin. He was in a suit looking formal and serious and ordinary and dead, as dead people do, which didn't seem right. Sam would have wanted to be dressed in a Batman costume or something. He would have wanted fireworks planted in his corpse to go off right when his coffin hit the bottom of his grave.

I could have talked to Sam's family but I felt like I already knew what answers they'd have for me.

"He was depressed."

"He was troubled."

"He just didn't get the help he needed."

Those were stupid answers. Just because an answer is right doesn't mean it's not stupid.

We all went down to the graveyard—me, Sam's girlfriend, Sam's corpse, who-ever else—for him to get put into the ground. The cold, dry autumn air had killed all of the grass. We all stood around Sam's hole as the coffin was lowered in and suddenly I thought that this was it: Sam's fist was going to burst out through the wooden top of his casket. He was going to clamber out with a party hat on, kick his girlfriend in the stomach for the sheer hell of it, flick a switch and the solo to "Stairway to Heaven" would start playing while he walked off back to his house laughing his head off.

His parents were sobbing as they lowered him in. I searched out Sam's girlfriend to see if she was crying, too. She wasn't. I wondered if some manual laborers were going to come in while we were still standing there and start throwing dirt over Sam right in front of us. They didn't. It was over. Sam was gone.

It was her hair that made me do it.

After Sam got put into the ground everyone dispersed but didn't leave. They milled around the graveyard like they were expecting something else to happen, except for Sam's girl. She was making a beeline toward the parking lot. She wasn't fast enough; I intercepted her.

I asked her, "What's with the hair?"

She looked around as though she were hoping for an escape route. "What?" she said.

"Your hair. You've dyed it."

"Yes. Yes I have."

"It's only been three days," I said.

"Oh, God," she said. "Please don't do this. Not here." She made to walk past me but I sidestepped into her path.

"Hold up!" I said. "Hold the fuck up!"

She stopped. I could feel the stares of the other funeral-goers directed toward us.

"Three days," I said. "It hasn't even been three days. Why did you dye your hair blonde? Why?"

"I . . . I don't know. What does that . . ." she stammered.

"You never cared. You never gave a shit. You are such a bitch."

"You're a total lunatic!" she said. "I can't believe you're doing this, and here, of all places. You're completely insane."

"What was wrong with him?" I exploded. "You were the only one who knew! Tell me what the fuck was wrong with him!"

"What do you mean? He was depressed. He had depression. He . . ."

"No, shut up. Shut up. That's a stupid answer."

"What the hell do you want me to say?"

"The punch." I shoved my hand in her face, tried to show her the two tiny scars that never healed after that night that I hit him. "Why'd he make me punch him? Who was he? Who the fuck was Sam?"

"You want to know why he made you hit him? It made him feel better. It helped him deal with pain. I don't know the answers to any of your other batshit crazy questions."

"You were the only one who knew him, don't you get it? You were the only one who really saw him like he was. You're the only one who has the whole narrative."

"You're out of your mind," Sam's girl said. "You're really this angry that Sam was never sad around you? He was doing you a favor. Jesus, of course he's not going to break down in front of you or show his cuts in front of you, you're his best friend. You were his best friend. He hid it for you. You weren't missing anything. You're such a fuck. You weren't missing anything."

"Cuts?" I said.

"Fuck you, by the way, for that phone call the night he died. Fuck you. And good job making a scene at your best friend's funeral in front of his family."

She started again toward her car, pushing past me.

"Cuts," I called after her, pleadingly. "What cuts?" But she was already too far away, out of my sight and gone.

It wasn't until after the funeral and a trip to the Internet that I learned that people can hide cuts in all sorts of interesting places: upper arms, thighs, ankles, abdomen, and hell, really, who is suddenly taken with the urge to inspect their friend's wrists? It's so hard to see something that you're not looking for, that you would never think to look for.

You were the only one who knew him, don't you get it? You were the only one who really saw him like he was. You're the only one who has the whole narrative.

Sam's girlfriend had given me something and it should have been enough but it wasn't. It was a symptom, something that a doctor writes on a sheet and puts in a folder, a bullet point. It didn't really mean anything. I needed Sam to wake from the dead and scrabble out of his grave and come find me. I needed him to show me the ghostly grey scars on his arms or torso or wherever, have him run his finger across each of them and tell me when and where they happened and then, maybe, possibly, I would be satisfied.

I didn't even know if Sam liked eating at McDonald's or not. I didn't. He said he didn't. When we figured out that the Secret Sauce was just Thousand Island dressing mixed with mayonnaise, Sam went outside and threw his Big Mac as hard as he could at the McDonald's window. It made a noise like a person hitting the ground from thirty-six stories up in the air. Yet we both kept going there. Why did we keep going there? When Sam got a job at McDonald's I found it so strange, so strange that he would make the center of his existence such a wretched and uncaring place. Masochist, I found myself thinking. A person who would subject himself to that kind of soul-crushing shit was a masochist, a self-hating lunatic, I had thought jokingly.

Sam ate Egg McMuffins. He said he could eat his weight in Egg McMuffins. I had only seen him eat a few, on those protracted drunken nights that gasped into the morning and demanded to be killed with fast food.

It never occurred to me that there could have been nights that he spent sad and awake as the morning came out to remind him of what was wrong with him, that he might have taken sad and ill-lit trips down that suburban road lined with those perpetually dead woods on his own. I didn't know how many Egg McMuffins Sam had eaten. I just didn't know.

It wasn't fair that he had killed himself. When we walked down that road we were in two entirely different places and I never knew it and it wasn't fair.

One day on the McDonald's route the incident with the Italians flashed darkly across my mind—Sam leading me down into some hallowed clearing by what, what did he say, divine intervention. Bullshit.

I decided to retrace his steps. I got down close to the trees and tried to spot the trail through them, but their branches had meshed into a tattered curtain that obscured my view. Finally I tried simply crashing through some weaker-looking branches once, twice, three times.

Finally I burst through and I found myself on top of the trail, a miraculously open passage as though Sam had parted the trees with some warrant from God, leading into that large clearing where we had confronted the Italians. The forest floor was plated with autumn leaves and there was the conspicuous bump of a large tree stump right in the clearing's center. It looked terribly accommodating; I sat down on it to rest.

The leaves on the ground around the stump were beginning to decay. They had lost the flippant plumage of the fall, melted together into the uniform color of dying.

I picked one up by the stem and spun it around between two fingers. I looked closer at it. The leaf was spotted with bits of dry rust, perhaps easy to see when it was a more flagrant color but now camouflaged.

It was blood. I put my eyes back down toward the ground and saw something decidedly unnatural on the forest floor. I picked it up. A razor blade. It was tinged with the same rust as the leaf. I stared at it dumbly for a minute, my senses and thoughts shut off to everything but the physical presence of this blood-stained metal piece lying in the palm of my hand.

This was what Sam did. I was overcome with the urge to know what it was like. Sam was dead. I couldn't ask him about it.

It hurt like all of massive hell, hurt so badly that I couldn't even make it all the way from the left side of my arm to the right. I had to stop halfway and I was left with an awful leaking line of wound that pattered blood onto the ground between my feet.

I looked at it as it bled. The blood squeezed its way out of the bottom of the cut in fat beads like tears.

Will Schutt
A Kind of Poetry

Sometimes you turn to poetry
the way you turn to another country.
Everything is better, more humane.
You notice things you wouldn't
otherwise. You notice things.
Watching gardeners trim
branches for birds to fly through
reminds you of holes in your own country's
trees, which only make room
for wires. The entire center perforated
like a dart board in a dive bar.
After awhile, however, you recall
those wires carry a language you know.

American Window Dressing

Half a dozen *pestemals* hanging on hooks,
    a cuckoo clock twigged from scrap metal,
a single copy of *Everyman's Haiku*—
    the letters pit the cover's look-at-me
moon sheen—and the poems I love
    inside: spartan, semitransparent, nature's fools,
like faraway countries in full disclosure.

"Put everything into it." My father's
    words on Sunday visits. Man of few words.
Those were the days work took him
    as far as Chungking and he sported
a straight green army coat he called
    his Mao Suit. His hair was still parted
straight to one side and he could still

lift me up so that I stood eyelevel
      with row after row of ducks in the restaurant
windows off Confucius Plaza, like
      smokers' lungs—thick tar up top swizzed
into brown and rose gold. A metal sling
      dug under their wings
ended in a hole the heads were put through.

Knowledge of them was terrible.
      Everything looked terrible: the heads
of bok choy noosed in rubber bands
      and pale-eyed fish laid out on ice. Terrible
things put delicately, like polite fictions
      families invent. The words stand behind
great portals and are seen, yet untouchable.

Camels

Whenever I say "equals"
you think of the little guy
no one's put down roses for
but all of us pay to have
our plot shoveled and are left
at best with wistful hope
someone will get the dates right,
someone do the heavy lifting,
someone square the bills.
The little white cup I drink coffee from
accumulates Camel stubs
burnt to the top of each camel's
hump, signs of an idle
retrospective style, pouring
one's life into long books
when work's dried up.
For mulling over his own face,
the camel has to hoof
his hump from this end to that.
Labor is the crop of his learning.
Just today I come across
three new novels all authored
by Bartleby, the Scrivener.

After *A Silvia*

MIRAVO IL CIEL SERENO,
LE VIE DORATE E GLI ORTI,
E QUINCI IL MAR DA LUNGI, E QUINDI IL MONTE —GIACOMO LEOPARDI

Remember? You used to thumb
through the pages of *Seventeen*
eyeing every snapshot of other
girls on the slopes of girlhood.
The song you sang at school
drifted through the quiet rooms
and out to the street. Vague, whatever-will-be,
May took up the air. I dropped
my books. I shoved my papers in a drawer—
half my life sewn shut inside
my father's house—and cupped my ear
to catch the sound of your voice
as you hauled your heavy workload home.
I'd look out at the clear sky,
the bright streets, people's yards,
all the way down to the sea
and all the way up the hillside.
No words really fit what I felt.
The hopeful pitch of then.
To think of it now tightens my chest
and grief ploughs through me.
Shock & blowback, tricks & masks—

why is it nothing keeps its word?
What's with all the lights burning in the distance?
Before winter starved the grass
or some compliment was paid
your modest, nothing-special looks,
some narrow sickness buried you.
Whatever boyhood I had
fate hijacked too. Old friend, is this that
world we stayed awake all night for?
Truth dropped in. Far off,
your cool hand points the way.

Brilliant Farewells

Toodle-oo is one way
bad guys and Frenchmen

bid goodbye, and adieu
tends to touch a chord

in nostalgists and strangers.
You can't leave for one place

without appearing
above or beneath another

yet the right valedictions
like refrains and high-fives

pave an expedient route
to come away with a way back.

"Sayonara, little sister."
"Time to go, buffalo."

Something extra should be said
for putting lamps out

with a long steel pole
beside a *quai*. Realists know

the rain suits others since
nothing need be said in the rain.

Ed. Diego Trelles Paz
The Future Is Not Ours

By Marion Wyce

Recently I found myself in a first-class seat on a flight to Philadelphia. Normally when I travel, I am seated somewhere deep in the bowels of the plane, so as I always do when I'm in an unfamiliar place, I catalogued my surroundings, the little details the airline had decided upon as signifiers of a first-class experience. There was the bathroom up front that was reserved solely for our use, as the flight attendant informed the other passengers over the PA system. There was the cloth napkin she used to cover my tray table during the meal service—for that matter, the mere fact that there was a meal, and that it was actually edible, was itself a differentiator. But what stood out to me most was when the two flight attendants, a man and a woman, drew themselves behind a little curtain. Being nosy almost by constitution, I shifted in my seat and craned my neck to peer through the gap in the curtain. And that's when I made my discovery: They were eating.

I spent much of the rest of the plane ride, in my extra wide, pleather seat, thinking about what it meant that the airline executives thought they needed to hide their employees' basic human needs from me. The curtain was there to protect me from seeing that they were just like me.

It was on that flight that I began reading *The Future Is Not Ours: New Latin American Fiction*, an anthology of stories by twenty-three writers born between 1970 and 1980. First published as an electronic anthology by a Colombian magazine in 2007, then as a print anthology by an Argentine publishing house in 2009,

Translated from Spanish by Janet Hendrickson. Rochester, NY: Open Letter, 2012.

these stories are frequently grim, even disturbing meditations on what it means to be human in an absurd and dehumanizing world. The editor is Diego Trelles Paz, born in 1977 in Peru, who has published the short story collection *Hudson el redentor* and the novel *El círculo de los escritores asesinos* and is a professor of Latin American literature and cinema at Binghamton University, State University of New York. In his introduction, Paz refers to the cynical disillusionment writers of his generation are known for, and many of the cultural moments he references are touchstones of my own adolescence and young adulthood, having been born in 1975: the fall of the Berlin Wall, the Tiananmen Square massacre, the collapse of the Soviet Union, the attack on the Twin Towers, the torture at Guantanamo. But as an American I've been relatively sheltered from these upheavals, with the exception of 9/11, experiencing them only as images on television or words in the newspaper. The writers in this anthology, Paz notes, were largely educated under the framework of military dictatorships, and many of their countries were ravaged by poverty, drug trafficking, and political repression during their formative years. Paz is interested in the way his contemporaries "face the act of writing" and describes the anthology as, among other things, "a response to a series of misconceptions associated with a demagogic idea, a slogan, proclaimed and repeated to the point of exhaustion, that the future belongs to the young." Above all, there's a strong current of violence throughout the anthology, but the effect isn't like being a spectator to Hollywood violence, which is performed for your titillation. Rather, the violence in these stories is almost mundane, and what's revealed is often both horrible and yet as ordinary and ultimately human as the two flight attendants behind the curtain, having their lunch.

Pintor, the narrator of Daniel Alarcón's piercing story, "Lima, Peru, July 28, 1979," has been killing dogs and stringing them up on lampposts during the earliest days of the Shining Path movement. He struggles to explain why, alternating between genuine pain and bemused cynicism: "You should know that I felt nothing for the dog other than steely blue-black hatred. I was cold and angry. Hurt by too many German philosophers in translation. Wounded by watching my father go blind beneath great swaths of leather, bending and manipulating each until, like magic, a belt, or a saddle, or a soccer ball appeared. Frustrated by an absurd evening spent killing and painting for the revolution." Elias, the protagonist of Argentinian writer Oliverio Coelho's "Sun-Woo," has a similar befuddlement about his own behavior and motivations. During a visit to Seoul, he has a sexual encounter with a young woman named Sun-Woo, a stranger he meets in a restaurant. She seems like a fantasy he has conjured, until he realizes she has locked him in her apartment as her prisoner, with no way to escape. She disappears for days and returns on a schedule obvious only to her, leaving Elias naked on her floor, contemplating the particulars of his life: "How long had it been since he had bathed? How long since he had opened a book? How long since he had cried? He had never cried for a woman in his life." The sex Elias has with Sun-Woo is violent; she injures him, possibly breaking his hip. Yet she has made him feel something, so it's painful for Elias the final time she leaves: "When he understood that this time Sun-Woo hadn't locked the door, he knelt down to cry."

In several stories, the writers go even further than detachment; the self is obliterated altogether. In "34," a story by Chilean writer Alejandro Zambra, the students at a prestigious school are referred to only by the number the teacher assigns them, which corresponds to their placement in alphabetical order. There are chilling echoes of Pinochet's reign, of course, in which state-sanctioned institutions can make people disappear altogether. The story's title character finds himself held back in school, a fact which changes his entire identity, yet he accepts it with resignation: "I appreciate your concern for me, but 34 no longer exists, he said. Now I'm 29, and I should get used to my new reality." Identity is fraught in these stories; the self can be swallowed up, or it can expand to consume others. "Family Tree" by Andrea Jeftanovic tells of a father whose young daughter works relentlessly to seduce him after her mother abandons them. The girl is described as his aggressive pursuer, almost as though he is a victim, yet she is the one who disappears when they eventually begin a sexual relationship and he sees only himself, reflected: "On top of her, looking into those gray eyes, which were my gray eyes. I was kissing myself. I was caressing my own marked bones, I ran against my own aquiline nose, I traced my narrow forehead."

As reflected in the anthology's title, there is little hope or redemption in these stories, no glimmer of a better future. Their power lies instead in an unswerving insistence on telling the full truth of being human: the darkness and ugliness that resides within us, the daily incongruities that we ignore in order to make sense of our lives, and, above all, the desire for self-determination. One of the stories that stayed with me long after I finished reading the book was "Any Old Story" by Guatemalan writer Ronald Flores. His protagonist gets no more than the pronoun *she*, and the very title of the story both draws attention to its unremarkable nature while also reminding me how disturbing it is that pain can ever seem unremarkable. In many ways, it's an old story: a young girl heads to the city, looking for something better: "She left town to improve herself, to become somebody[...] She knew that if she stayed any longer, her fate would be next to the fire, making tortillas, bearing children until her body dried up, keeping vigil through her husband's drunken nights, and enduring his beatings." She ends up working in a sweatshop, then raped by the foremen, then pregnant and fired in disgrace despite having done nothing wrong. In the story's final two sentences—her only spoken lines—she gets a say in her future, and what she finally imagines is her own erasure. She tells her cousin, "'If they ask for me, tell them that you haven't seen me; the city swallowed me up. Make up any old story.'"

Catherine Barnett
The Game of Boxes

By F. Daniel Rzicznek

As a writer, I create yearlong, but because of my position as an instructor of English composition, summer remains my season of "play," three months when I treat writing like a full-time job. The giddiness of this freedom echoes back to my distant but distinct existence before summer jobs like golf caddying, dishwashing, bagging groceries, and even, one summer, unloading trucks, ushered me into the workforce. I find that this sense of play remains urgent, even essential, to my own work, but, more pressingly, to the books I choose to read. The spare, yet intricate poems in Catherine Barnett's second full-length collection, *The Game of Boxes*, fulfill this need for linguistic and imaginative diversion. She is concerned with how we talk to our gods, our parents, our children, and our lovers. Reading Barnett's work feels, happily, like play as it breaks through inattention and ennui to refigure the familiar in terms so original they become alien.

The book's opening section offers more than a dozen poems with the title "Chorus," most of them invoking a collective "we." In the "Chorus" poem beginning "We thought it was safe under trees," a storm overhead sweeps away an onlooker's scarf, which Barnett describes as "red like a toy." What type of toy, exactly, is withheld, the result being a controlled ambiguity that reverses expectations. To say a storm lifts and moves something as if it were a toy would be using a threadbare simile, but Barnett has switched movement for color—just one of many times in the collection that my anticipations were refreshingly thwarted. Barnett approaches

Minneapolis, MN: Graywolf Press, 2012.

language as a flexible, malleable material to work with, as opposed to a set of fixed or inherited formulas. In fact, it seems to be the formulaic that the poems want to undermine via play, as in "Sojourn," which presents an autobiographical speaker having her picture taken by her son. The son is unhappy with the photo and asks playfully *"Do it again* [. . .] *Pretend you're really climbing"* and the poet, upon seeing the second version, is unsure if her eye is "smiling or crying," creating more of that ambiguity. It is an unlikely place to end, and this is one of many poems in the book that employs non-closure (charged with negative capability) to punctuate the personal lyric. *Nothing ends neatly—get used to it*, I can almost hear the work saying beneath its breath. Later in the book, the poem "Providence" begins, "This evening I shared a cab with a priest," the setup to a million jokes about religion, ethics, and mortality, but this particular priest reveals that "Some of the best sermons / don't have endings," a possibility that Barnett's attractive and challenging work hinges upon.

Amidst poems that consider both literal and spiritual states of parent-child duality, twenty-four short lyrics (all collected in their own section under the title "sweet double, talk-talk") explore love and sex with more fresh turns and moments of surprise. In the poem beginning "Sure, I say, fine, as if it doesn't matter," Barnett delivers a metaphor to impart the pleasure of a lover's touch: "a match lifted from its neat white box / and struck on the afterlife bed." The phrase "afterlife bed" pushes the reader back to the poems' subject (the physical act of sex) while adding the strangely abstract modifier "afterlife," a leap that successfully builds on the poetic momentum created by the unexpected "struck match" metaphor. Later, in "I want to see his face," the speaker's lover is "skipping rocks across a grave / or swinging his legs at its edge." These images defy common sense (as well as accuracy of action), which help create halting, haunting visuals. Another poem from the same series begins, "Though I can't sleep neither could I wake," a tense shift so subtle that it might slip right by. But it underlines the poet's awareness of consciousness (dreaming is its own peculiar and unconscious form of play, memory and our conception of the past being another) and leaves unclear where and when the poem takes place.

Confronted once more with a suspension of finality, I'm reminded that Barnett's poems fail to make "sense" in order to reflect a world that fails, too, to convincingly manufacture closure. The last poem in "sweet double, talk-talk" begins "Then he whispers *there, there* as if I were a child / and not a woman lying beside him // but what's wrong with that." *The Game of Boxes* reminds us that even grownups are still capable of fear, wonder, confusion, anger, joy, lust, and desire, and that in a mass culture rife with false resolution and happy endings, poetry can provide the necessary weight to return us to terra firma and the complicated, unceasing task of being human: a task that requires compassion, improvisation, and acceptance of the uncertain; a task that asks for a bit of innocence, even ignorance—in other words, a bit of play.

J.G. Farrell
The Singapore Grip

By Drew Calvert

The Singapore Grip is the final installment of J.G. Farrell's "Empire Trilogy," which chronicles the spectacle of British colonialism over the course of two centuries, from Ireland to India to Southeast Asia. It is also one of the only Anglo-American works of fiction set primarily in the city in which I grew up. I discovered it over a decade ago on the shelves of a secondhand bookstore in a corner of Far East Plaza, these days one of downtown Singapore's lesser shopping malls. The bookstore was popular among Singaporean university students looking for discount study guides, backpackers swapping travelogues, and expatriate wives searching for profiles of philanthropists and monks.

I noticed the book on the shelf but never bothered to inspect its cover; it sounded like an account of geopolitical strategy or a moist homage to British glory. It did not occur to me that *The Singapore Grip* (New York Review Books Classics, 2005) could be a work of literature, because in that stage of my life, I'd come to believe that literature took place in London or New York, not Singapore. With the exception of Vietnam War stories, I had not read any English-language literature with Southeast Asia as its principle subject. What I had read were coffee-table books of Cambodian ruins, predictable pseudo-spiritual travelogues, gap-year tales of hallucinogens and snake blood, the columns of globalization buffs like Thomas Friedman and Fareed Zakaria, and the memoirs of Lee Kuan Yew. In English class, George Orwell was introduced as the author of *Nineteen Eighty-Four*, not a lapsed imperialist who fled British India; Anthony Burgess was the author of *A Clockwork Orange*, not *The Malayan Trilogy*, a comic novel set in pre-independence Malaysia.

When I left Singapore at eighteen, I searched other literary traditions for the deep reservoir of wisdom I felt I had missed in that materialistic, utilitarian, thoroughly corporate city-state. I studied Russian, I read as widely as possible in the American tradition; in 2008, I moved to China and taught English literature to a small group of university students. It was in Beijing, at the height of the financial crisis, that I began to wonder whether I had lived through a unique historical period, one in which the American Empire had reached its zenith and begun its slow collapse. Every so often a detail would flare up from memory: In 1998, while a financial crisis wreaked havoc on the economies of Southeast Asia and the streets of Jakarta filled with protesters, I overheard a man wearing a Cornell tee shirt in the lobby of a five-star hotel say: "This is the time to buy those Indonesian puppets." In 2000, a Filipina maid jumped from the balcony of an expatriate high-rise building. At the bars along the Singapore River, US sailors discussed Thai women and oil traders discussed their companies' assets over mugs of Tiger beer. A classmate of mine from the international school once stole the towel of a Bangladeshi construction worker while he showered in a public restroom. (In retrospect, the misbehavior of American teenagers seems closely aligned with neoliberal economics: it's all about what you can get away with.) Because I lacked a sound ideology, these memories had no organizing principle; they remained minor traumas and curiosities.

Even after I decided that the multicultural arcadia of my youth was in many respects a sham (some journalists began calling it "Disneyland with the death penalty"), I still had an inexplicable desire to belong there, even if only in memory. This ambivalence has the potential to be toxic. Despite his keen sense of social justice, George Orwell was occasionally nostalgic for Anglo-India, and while this seems to have afforded him certain insights into authoritarian personalities, it was also clearly a source of debilitating shame. *Burmese Days*, Orwell's most thorough (and mostly autobiographical) account of on-the-ground imperialism, is powerful and clear-eyed, but leaves its readers without a shred of hope.

Earlier this year I took a trip to Penang, the first British colony in Malaysia, and it was there that I finally read *The Singapore Grip*. Its effect is different from *Burmese Days*. It is much funnier, and also more "literary," in the sense that it is less polemical. Farrell lampoons the absurdity of the British colonial experience in Singapore, but he does so with a fanatical attention to detail and a keen historical perspective, thus implicating his Anglo-American readers in something more corrupt than the hypocrisies of businessmen and their disappointing progeny (one of whom makes the wonderful mistake of inviting a yogi to a company jubilee). It is clear that Farrell is not a cheerleader for Britain's governance model and economic policy. Still, he does not build an allegorical framework in order to codify its injustices on strictly ideological grounds; instead, he describes the entire mess.

He also assigns himself the dual role of historian and storyteller, with a narrative voice that falls somewhere between Monty Python and Tolstoy. In the first chapter, he writes that Singapore's "founder," Sir Stanford Raffles, "was by no means the lantern-jawed individual you might have expected: indeed, a rather vague-looking man in a frock coat," then follows this up with a thirty-page profile of the colonial rubber industry. Near the end of the novel, before he describes the gruesome murder of Chinese citizens at the hands of occupying Japanese soldiers, he reminds readers in an aside that the Tanglin golf course was blessed with "respectable greens." *The Siege of Krishnapur*, the second volume of the trilogy, is filled with descriptions of Indian weather in the same ironic mode ("Picture a map of India as a big tennis court with two or three hedgehogs crawling over it . . . each hedgehog might represent one of the dust storms which during the summer wander aimlessly here and there over the Indian plains"), but the weather has dire consequences. Farrell's strategy of oscillating between satire and epic does not allow for complacent reading. Just when readers of *The Singapore Grip* think they can settle into a comic novel of matters, history intervenes in the form of a Japanese airstrike:

> The first bomb landed in the long-disused swimming pool sending up a great column of water which hung in the air for a moment like a block of green marble before crashing down again. Another bomb landed simultaneously in the road, blowing a snowstorm of red tiles off the Mayfair's roof and out over the compound, and another in the grove of old rubber which lay between the Mayfair and the Blackett's house.

More than anything, what makes this novel powerful is that it goes in search of what is elemental about the era it describes. Beneath the irony is a genuine curiosity about the details of human life that are occulted within the historical process. Farrell himself once explained his literary impulse by pointing out that "history leaves out the most important thing of all: the detail of what being alive is like."

First published in 1978, *The Singapore Grip* is full of contemporary echoes: petty egos deciding the fates of nations, Quran burnings followed by riots, Sinophilia and Sinophobia, the anxiety of Western intellectuals, the excesses of capitalism, a sickening military-industrial complex. The title is a reference to a phenomenon rumored to be central to the "colonial experience" but that remains a mystery to Matthew Webb, young Oxford graduate, likely inheritor of his father's rubber empire, vegetarian, naïve defender of the League of Nations, and proponent of international brotherhood. He arrives in Singapore a few years before Japanese bombs begin to fall on Bukit Timah. The conceit of *The Singapore Grip*—which refers to an erotic act popular among prostitutes but is variously interpreted as a secret communist handshake, a disease, a cocktail, a macroeconomic anomaly, a mode of governance, a hairpin, or a rattan-style handbag ("like a Shanghai basket, but smaller")—is timeless in the way it reveals the symbols that compose a social hierarchy. In fact, if you changed a few words, the novel could pass for a send-up of contemporary expatriate life in Southeast Asia, with its sense of entitlement ("To the indignation of Tanglin the Cold Storage had stopped baking white bread"), spiritual bankruptcy ("Who's going to die for the stock exchange?") and the para-dox of insisting on timeless normalcy while indulging in paranoia ("Could you be altogether certain that you would not find yourself sharing your soufflé with a Japanese parachutist?"). And it foreshadows, too, the tendency among contem-porary Western executives in Asia to interpret their global deal making and price fixing as cross-cultural exchange. Before there were CEOs quoting from the *Sunzi* to explain their enlightened strategy of underpaying workers in Guangzhou, there were executives who saw that "Oriental" authoritarian power could be an asset to their firms. Farrell manages to capture this in a single brief episode:

> Yes, Gordon Bennett had recognized in the Sultan a really high-class person, and the Sultan, for his part, he felt sure, had not altogether failed to notice his own qualities of good breeding. Not long before, so he had heard, a guest of the Sultan, a titled English lady, had expressed a caprice to swim in the shark-infested Strait of Johore. For many a host this would have been too much, but not for the Sultan. What had he done? He had instructed several hundred of his palace guards to enter the water and link hands to form a shark-proof enclosure in which the lady could safely bathe. That, Bennett knew, was class. He could tell a classy act a mile off.

But there is one way in which the novel is timeless: it reveals the arbitrary nature of our identities, affections, and convictions. It does not propose a solution to the injustice inherent in colonial (or postcolonial) economies; it does not offer an uplift-ing message of liberty or solidarity. It merely invites readers to consider the fact that the world is full of people we might have been. By investing creative energy in his character's illusions, Farrell is able to show us how easily we might have been, for example, a French diplomat with little to do but polish his monocle, a Malay rubber planter, an idealistic Oxford type who clings to international justice "like barnacles clinging to the hull of a sinking ship," a jitterbugging Filipino aristocrat, a Chinese shop owner, an American writing an exposé on the indignities of pineapple canning, or a Eurasian housekeeper who speaks her own incomprehensible dialect. This is the quality that separates the novelist from the historian, the writer from the polemicist. Nobody writes a trilogy of novels simply to prove a point. It requires a particular kind of curiosity and a persistent imagination, what Nabokov once called "insubordination in its purest form."

I read *The Singapore Grip* at a hostel along Love Lane, the same narrow street Sir Stanford Raffles stayed on during his first visit to Penang in 1805. When I was finished reading, I visited the museums. I read a letter written by a Malay spiritual leader attacking the British East India Company and the irredeemable decadence of Western civilization. I scanned the photographs of Sun Yat Sen during his tour through Southeast Asia to raise funds for the Chinese revolution. And late that afternoon I found myself standing in the preserved, pre-independence bedroom of a Malaysian-Chinese teenager, staring at a pair of bejeweled wedding slippers enclosed in a fine glass case. The house had Scottish stained-glass windows, a stately Confucian dining room, and bright Malay fabrics hanging from the walls. It occurred to me that what distinguishes Farrell's novel is its fascination with how a series of details can undermine the version of history we want to believe. And it gave me hope to think that even a satirist relies on that mysterious human impulse for which a pair of wedding slippers is as interesting as an empire.

Elena Ferrante
My Brilliant Friend

By Martha Witt

American readers are likely to have strong olfactory associations with the southern Italy glorified by travel and restaurant guides, where the cuisine is rich, the markets overflowing, and where women patiently tend simmering pots for long stretches of the day. In *My Brilliant Friend*, the first installment in her forthcoming trilogy, Elena Ferrante beautifully manipulates the olfactory to deliver its underbelly—a world on the outskirts of 1950s Naples drenched in a "stink" that binds hunger, fear, violence, and female rage.

Elena Greco, the narrator of *My Brilliant Friend*, is sixty-six when we meet her in a brief prologue in which she receives a phone call from her best friend's son, Rino. During this phone call, we learn that Lila Cerullo, Elena's best friend from childhood, has "vanished." Elena is not surprised, nor does she tell Rino, that his mother is fulfilling a longstanding promise to vanish without a trace. In fact, Elena shares the information only with the reader and then sets out to write the book that will ostensibly explain Lila's disappearance. Elena Greco begins with a description of how she met Lila when they were little girls playing with dolls. Before they even speak to each other, Lila takes Elena's doll and casts it into the basement of Don Achille, the man who, in the imagination of the town's children, is the ogre ready to tear a child apart limb by limb. In one bold move, Elena throws Lila's doll after her own, and then Lila leads Elena into that basement—the first of many horrifying journeys, both real and metaphorical, that the two girls will take over the course

Translated from Italian by Ann Goldstein. New York: Europa Editions, 2012.

of this narrative spanning the next twelve years of their lives. Elena's deep and abiding friendship with Lila is often fraught with envy and pain intertwined with admiration. But any alliance is crucial to the physical and mental survival of these two girls, trapped in a world infested by a rage that—in their town—manifests as a particularly female disease:

> As a child I imagined tiny, almost invisible animals that arrived in the neighborhood at night, they came from the ponds, from the abandoned train cars beyond the embankment, from the stinking grasses called *fetenti*, from the frogs, the salamanders, the flies, the rocks, the dust, and entered the water, the food, and the air, making our mothers, our grandmothers as angry as starving dogs. They were more severely infected than the men, because while men were always getting furious, they calmed down in the end; women, who appeared to be silent, acquiescent, when they were angry flew into a rage that had no end.

As in Ferrante's past novels, particularly *Troubling Love* (2006) and *Days of Abandonment* (2005), the mother-daughter bond is freighted with pain, misunderstanding, and shame. At every critical juncture in Elena's life, her mother threatens to pull her into the muck of the world that she is trying so desperately to escape. When Elena is accepted to middle school, her mother complains about the cost and wants her to forgo schooling and stay home to help with the house. Elena's father is more supportive, and with the intervention of Elena's teacher, her mother gradually relents and Elena is allowed to pursue her education. Lila, despite her brilliance, is not so lucky. After elementary school, her parents refuse to allow her to test for middle school. They keep her home, and she goes to work in her father's shoe shop. In the afternoons, she sneaks out to study with Elena, who is astounded by her autodidacticism. It turns out that, with the help of library books, Lila has been keeping up with all of the subjects Elena is studying in middle school. Incredibly, Lila's knowledge still surpasses Elena's in every subject.

Foregrounding the girls' passion for knowledge are the many thwarted passions of the women surrounding them: there is the woman who has gone crazy from loving a philandering poet, the neighbor who regularly beats her children, the women who attack each other on the street. In fact, at the root of the great tension that propels this narrative forward lies the girls' fear of merging into the looming female world that beckons them. Although they cannot articulate this fear, the girls eventually create a term for it. Elena writes, "The thing was happening to (Lila) that I mentioned and that later she called dissolving margins. It was—she told me—as if, on the night of a full moon over the sea, the intense black mass of a storm advanced across the sky, swallowing every light, eroding the circumference of the moon's circle, and disfiguring the shining disk, reducing it to its true nature of rough, insensate material."

This riveting narrative, which derives its tension from language and emotion rather than plot, demands a wordsmith as translator; fortunately, Ann Goldstein, who has translated Ferrante's previous novels, brings to the English version the skills to transmit the subtle but crucial tension of the original. Issues of translation, and Elena's own function as translator, are, in fact, intimately intertwined with her coming-of-age, academic blossoming, and eventual escape from the fate of her peers. Italian is the scholastic language of Elena's world, the language of the teachers, of television, and national politics. But *Napolitano* (Neapolitan dialect) is her native tongue, the language of the town, the less educated and, of course, of the *Camorra* (the southern Italian version of the Mafia). Throughout the text, Elena is in the position of "translating" from Neapolitan into Italian for the reader, and she becomes increasingly aware of the ever growing divide between speakers of Italian and Neapolitan.

Since the author and the narrator of *My Brilliant Friend* share the same first name and origins, it is enticing to read this narrative as an autobiographical account of growing up female and poor in post-war Naples. But the impulse to merge biography and fiction is particularly irksome in the case of Elena Ferrante, who many suspect is not even a woman but writer and journalist Domenico Starnone. Despite film adaptations of her novels, high critical acclaim, and numerous recognitions, including the much sought-after Elsa Morante prize for literature, Elena Ferrante never makes public appearances and has only granted a few interviews via e-mail. The elusiveness of her identity has created such a stir throughout Italy that cynics have decreed it a publicity stunt. Ferrante, on the other hand, argues that her anonymity is an effort to separate the self she is "in life" from her "writing self" in an attempt to be as true to the latter as possible. In fact, *My Brilliant Friend* is very much a book about identity and the particularly female struggle to protect and nurture a self robust enough to hold out against the barrage of forces that threaten to eclipse it.

As in Ferrante's previous work, identity becomes increasingly defined by physical appearances. As Elena and Lila reach adolescence, Elena compares herself unfavorably to Lila, though she is also aware that her friend's beauty is partly responsible for eclipsing her ambitions and intelligence. The more beautiful Lila becomes, the more she must devote her energy and wit to self-protection and fending off men's sexual attractions and jealousies. In order to avoid the attentions of one rich young suitor that her family encourages but who is particularly reprehensible to Lila, she turns her attentions to the local grocer, Stefano. At sixteen years old, Lila marries Stefano. Though Lila is seemingly reconciled to her domestic role, through Elena, we continue to catch whiffs of the brilliant, outrageous girl of the early chapters who promises to return in electrifying, unexpected ways. After all, as a small child, Lila Cerullo birthed her own self into literacy:

> Then the teacher turned to Lila and with sincere admiration asked her in front of all of us, 'Who taught you to read and write, (Lila) Cerullo?' Cerullo, that small dark-haired, dark-eyed child, in a dark smock with a red ribbon at the neck, and only six years old, answered, 'Me.'

While contending with an identity defined by those around her, Lila, like her creator, nurtures another self that insists on shaping the language and structure through which it will flourish.

Karl Ove Knausgaard
My Struggle, Book One

By Josh Billings

Karl Ove Knausgaard's *My Struggle* is one of those rare books that appears at first to be failing miserably at what a novel is supposed to do, but then turns out by its end to have succeeded, remarkably, at something new. Its syrup-slow narrative avoids the big-things-happen-then-bigger-things-happen rhythm of a Hollywood movie; at the same time, it isn't quite meaning-averse enough to qualify for the self-conscious atmospherics of a novel in which "nothing happens." Nothing does happen in *My Struggle*. Not all at once, but gradually, like the erosion of a gigantic cliff. What gives the novel its tension is that the worst part of its disaster always seems about to happen. This overwhelming sense of dread transforms a typical coming-of-age story into a monster movie—or, to put it another way, it shows us that childhood is itself a monster movie. This feeling of imminent danger is part of what makes growing up such a scary process—but it also charges the world, filling experiences that we will later dull with an almost (to our older selves, at least) unbearable significance. Here, for example, is a brief description of the narrator Karl Ove's first love, with a girl named Hanne: "I was only thinking about Hanne, even though she was sitting in the same room as I was. Or was it thinking? . . . it was more as if I were full to the brim with emotions which did not leave any space for thought. And so it remained for the whole of the winter and spring." He continues, "Every morning I awoke and looked forward to going to school, where she would be. If she wasn't there, if she was ill or out of town, all meaning immediately

Translated from Norwegian by Don Bartlett. Brooklyn, NY: Archipelago Books, 2012.

drained out of everything, the rest of the day was just a question of endurance. For what? What was I waiting for while I was waiting?" Knausgaard's last question here perfectly captures the appeal of *My Struggle*, a book that ultimately seems to be about nothing more, or less, than "waiting." There is a creative writing maxim that instructs the writer to take his time getting to the climax of a scene and then, once that climax has been reached, to get out. Knausgaard does this one better by getting out before he has even gotten in. The young Karl Ove sits in his classroom thinking about Hanne a few desks away . . . and then suddenly two whole seasons have passed, and he is in love. The climax of the story—the one that I had been growing more and more anxious for as Karl Ove's glances grew more desperate—is omitted, meaning that, on a narrative level at least, it is not important, or at least no more important than anything else.

Performed only occasionally, such antidramatics would feel accidental, but Knausgaard's persistence raises them to the level of method, creating a world in which to see is to write, and to write requires a constant combination of order and chaos. "For several years I had tried to write about my father," the narrator says at one point. "But had gotten nowhere, probably because the subject was too close to my life, and thus not so easy to force into another form, which of course is a prerequisite for literature." A few sentences later he adds, "Writing is more about destroying than creating." *Form* and *destruction*: the two words run like rails through *My Struggle*, creating an energy that we see not only in the writing itself, but in the book's central relationship between the jittery, unformed narrator and his rule-obsessed father. A powerful, but deeply frustrated patriarch, the older Knausgaard haunts his son's life both before and after his death. His alcoholic dissolution ends (for himself at least) in the inevitable tragedy, but for his sons, the suffering continues into an agonizing but also occasionally cathartic aftermath. Karl Ove and his brother are informed of their father's passing and then immediately called in to clean it up, which they do one room at a time, scrubbing and dumping and generally just reasserting some small order in the midst of what appears to be catastrophe.

They succeed, in the same way that Knausgaard has: by paying attention to the individual details of their world with such tenacity that eventually those details detach themselves from the surrounding chaos and become bricks in something new. What is that something? *My Struggle* is the first of six books in a cycle that Knausgaard has written (the only one so far translated into English, by Don Bartlett), a fact that would seem to urge caution on the reader overeager to trace its themes. But as Knausgaard himself reminds us continually, all readings (and writings) leave something out. The mysterious truth of this is easy to forget in a world where every new story burns to leapfrog its peers into the unquestionable realm of myth; but it's true nonetheless, in a way that anyone who's ever written a line, or a recipe, or told a joke can attest. Describe a death meticulously, down to the last shudder, and it will still not be death: it will be *dead*. Leave the right things out, on the other hand, and you might find yourself creating something even more startling: a book so shot through with emptiness and death that it leaves its readers feeling full and alive. A deeply morbid book, *My Struggle* is nonetheless as full of life as a boat is of wind or a house is of light.

Leslie Adrienne Miller
Y: Poems

By Callista Buchen

Leslie Adrienne Miller is fascinated with the male child's evolving sense of right and wrong, as well as his linguistic and physical development and the factors that shape these processes. The riveting poems of her new collection, *Y*, explore that fascination, bringing together a variety of disciplines around child development— biological, social, cultural, and parental. In the second poem of the collection, "The Lucifer Effect," we see the boy who appears throughout the collection interacting with a nearly blind neighbor who offers a treat through the fence: "Learning her limits is a game he suspects / he shouldn't play, but sometimes he's quiet / on purpose: some funny place in him likes / to see her struggle."

Miller synthesizes research from a long list of sources that treat subjects as radically diverse as boy sopranos, language acquisition, feral children, testicular distention, genes, gender, and art. Miller also includes "adversaria" sections, each on its own page, where she includes short, research-based passages, typographically and functionally different from the poems. The adversaria on page 16 concludes: "They were surprised to find / massive palindromes, hairpin-like structures / that contain DNA sequences that read the same / backward and forward. Are we not drawn onward / to a new Era? The system is robust, / and it doesn't depend on the weather." Explained in "A Note on the Adversaria," these moments "are almost all collaged direct quotes from sources listed at the back of the book and represent the poet's attempt to leave a trail of bread crumbs from her forays into disciplines

Minneapolis, MN: Graywolf Press, 2012.

beyond her own in search of answers to questions the poems themselves collectively ask and only provisionally answer." This strategy allows the poems and the adversaria, each of which are strong and compelling as individual pieces, to resonate even further as an ongoing dialogue.

In addition to collaging research, Miller's work deftly combines poetic strategies—the lyrical, narrative, reflective, and the new, in mostly traditional shapes—with precision and comprehensive intelligence. The resulting work is thoughtful, and visceral—readers will find both their minds and hearts engaged. Through the complex questions she articulates, Miller allows us to feel with the child and with his observer(s): "All fodder, fur, and fury, / he's bound to roll the sturdy carcass / of imperative against even this, / his glittering box of tokens for the heart."

Perhaps the greatest success of the collection is the organic ease with which Miller couples the extent and scope of the research with insistent and emotional inquiry. She builds a new whole in splicing these veins, allowing the project to wrestle with the relationship of parent to child and child to parent. For instance, in "Relinquishing the Fusional Moment," the speaker begins by identifying the changing child: "The first sign is his rejection / of the French lullabies. The second, / a predilection for meat, / three, standing up to pee." Later, the speaker acknowledges how these changes also propel a kind of relativity, forcing changes to the speaker's sense of position: "I'm becoming another planet fast, / a hurtling ball of foreign gases."

In poems like "Tuileries," Miller implicates the reader in the child's development, asking, of a scene of a child running at birds, "teeth bared with a brutal glee," "How is our laughter at this good?" Miller is unafraid to indict the reader and the child, suggesting that an essential quality is unacknowledged:

What power there is, children claim like a sweet,
a desire not grounded in need, but arriving
nonetheless in their consciousness,
an itch to rule even this make shift roost.

The speaker finds something of this experience in her adult self:

All I know is: were you to appear

in the garden at this moment as threat
to that boy body scooped from my own,
I too would wear such a face,
and I'd be aiming to kill.

Y wallops the reader with its quiet power, and of course it must, given that in reading the collection, "then we understand again that our minds / might not, after all, be our own to close." Leslie Adrienne Miller's investigation into development becomes an examination of the elusive slippage of relation and (seeming) opposition, one where art and science, fear and longing, love and distance coalesce and "form a cradle that frees // and captures all at once."

Per Petterson
It's Fine by Me

By Jeanne-Marie Jackson

In a 1981 essay that tries to salvage Realism from indefinability, literary critic Marshall Brown describes the technique of silhouetting. What makes the reality aesthetic feel so real, he says, is what he calls "the form of figure against ground." He means that in big novels by Great Writers about small things, the individual emerges like a cameo against a social backdrop. It is just this sort of contrast between character and milieu that I thought I was encountering in the brief first chapter of Per Petterson's novel *It's Fine by Me*.

We are introduced to our narrator, a thirteen-year-old boy named Auden Sletten, as he strides onto a playground and towards the seventh grade. He is avowedly alone. The scene is set for maximum distinction between this Oslo country kid and everyone else: "Through the windows I could see faces," he observes, "and those sitting on the inside pressed their noses against the panes and watched me standing in the rain." This description is typical of Auden's working-class Norway, where groups seem somehow impenetrable; they're set off against the vivid locales of adolescent isolation that form the story's spine. The schoolyard is just the first in a series of dim and dusty environments, wrested by Don Bartlett into pointed English prose: a dark bedroom, an old car, a cabin made of cardboard in the woods.

And yet Auden's alienation, his place as a cameo, gives way to a more crucial dimension of this not-quite-coming-of-age tale. The novel reads more as series of

Minneapolis, MN: Graywolf Press, 2012.

incandescent portraits of *other* estranged people. Auden comes to the fore but then recedes, evacuating his own sense of self to act as a stage for the stories around him (at one point we read that he does "not know who it is that he sees" in the mirror). His narrating consciousness foregrounds an astonishing range of characters—from a drunk, absent dad to the lame farmer who briefly fills his shoes—who emerge as if from a tableau as Auden shines a spotlight upon them.

The trajectory of Auden's growth is disrupted at every turn, so that we're forced to focus on the people who form him rather than on the process of his formation. We meet Auden at a disaffected thirteen and leave him at a slightly less disaffected eighteen, but see him at various points in between and as a young child being beaten by his father. In addition to the yoke of a few recurring characters like his best friend, the aspiring writer Arvid, these unplotted points are united through grief and the kindnesses that assuage it. Auden's younger brother drives a car into a river, but when Auden himself almost drowns he is rescued by a couple of generous strangers. In this way what seems like a desolate book is redeemed as an archive of luminous moments, some painful and some good.

In the last chapter of *It's Fine by Me* Auden's father also dies, years after his younger son, and Auden is literally left to pick up the pieces. "There wasn't much," he admits. "His knife, a few keys he had kept for long-forgotten doors, two fifty-kroner notes and a small black and white photograph." The woman in the photo is an old girlfriend who had gone to school with his parents, and Auden can do better than just carry her crumpled image in his pocket. Instead, he allows his mother to tell the story of three people who loved each other a long time ago. In this way, Petterson avoids the cynicism that a chronological narrative of Auden's wising up might have conjured. Life is often bad, but *It's Fine by Me* also allows space for when it isn't.

Benjamin Stein
The Canvas

By John King

Because the very act of reading Benjamin Stein's *The Canvas* involves metaphysical provocations, it defies any normal attempt at summarization or evaluation. I haven't had an experience like this since I read the 1994 English translation of George Perec's novel, *A Void*, which both in English and French contains no instance of the letter e. *The Canvas,* translated from the German with charming deftness by Brian Zumhagen, brings to American readers another great work in the European experimental tradition, experiments that tend to be very precise in their execution.

In the case of *The Canvas*, there are two sides, and whichever the reader chooses to read first will provide an entirely different sense of narrative tension. If this device were not precocious enough, the title page also suggests that the reader might want to read each chapter alternately, like a story that switches between plots. "Of course," Stein adds, "you're also free to find your own way."

I began with the half about Amnon Zichroni, an endearing Jewish boy who learns that he has the psychic ability to relive the memories of anyone he touches. As a boy, a mishap involving a purloined copy of *The Picture of Dorian Gray* sends him to Switzerland, and eventually, through his best efforts to understand the holy purpose of his secret ability, he becomes a psychologist, to help damaged people find their way back to themselves, and the world:

> In analysis, you could put the reins back in their hands—or rather, the pallet and the paintbrush, so they could set a new tone on the canvas of their memories.

Translated from German by Brian Zumhagen. Rochester, NY: Open Letter Books, 2012.

> You could even become a canvas yourself, a projection screen where the patients
> could sketch possible alternative portraits and try out new ways of entering into
> relationships with other people again.

Considering the thematic connections to Wilde's novel, this gift sometimes seems ominous.

Zichroni's calling becomes tragic when a journalist named Jan Wechsler questions the truth of an excavated repressed memory of someone whom Amnon had helped.

The other half of *The Canvas* tells at once a less mystical and more psychologically unsettling story. An airline delivers a suitcase to the publisher Jan Wechsler one Shabbos afternoon. (If the reader has already read the other half, then this portion of *The Canvas* makes the reader try to connect this character to the "journalist" Jan Wechsler who appeared cryptically in the first part, but such connections can only be made provisionally, and become more problematic as the "Jan Wechsler" portion continues.) Although the penmanship on the receipt seems like his, and the address is correct, the suitcase is not, to Jan's knowledge, his own. Before he allows himself to open the suitcase, Jan Wechsler takes the reader along several anecdotes from his life, including his peculiar relationship to books:

> After our move a few years ago, I came to a bitter realization: most of the books
> that I had imagined I owned had in reality never been my property. I had bor-
> rowed them, from friends and from libraries. They hadn't been with me for
> some time, only in my head, where memory rewrites everything and sometimes
> distorts it beyond recognition.

He lets a long time pass before examining the luggage, and when he does, his own identity begins to unravel. He finds books under his own name, and becomes convinced that there must be another Jan Wechsler, a writer, with whom the airline has apparently confused him. Over time, though, as his wife and children leave him, his certainty that he isn't the other Jan Wechsler deteriorates, and, like the alternative drafts that psychoanalysis provides to Zichroni's patients, Wechsler remembers more than one history for himself.

Wechsler keeps striving to reveal the true mystery of who he is. Is this schizophrenia, dementia, or perhaps a case of metaphysical doppelgängers? Which Wechsler, if any, is the real one? And does he exist perhaps in some ontological overlap with Zichroni himself? The confounding dual detours in Wechsler's memories resonate deeply, especially as the narrative masterfully reconstructs itself toward the end of the Wechsler half. *The Canvas* left me with a sense that if religion and literature both aim to understand human character, the struggle might never end:

> I have still only seen a fragment from the image of my past. The largest part is still covered with a black cloth. . . . But over there, in the water, is my lost self. It's waiting for me. I just have to reach for it.

In Benjamin Stein's hands, this struggle for identity is a terrifying, worthwhile fight. *The Canvas* is a mind-bending companion in the best possible sense.

The Shortlist

Danilo Kiš
The Attic

Translated from Serbian by John K. Cox. Champaign, IL: Dalkey Archive Press, 2012

It's slight in size, but *The Attic*, the 1962 debut novel by Danilo Kiš (famous for later works like *A Tomb for Boris Davidovich* and *Encyclopedia of the Dead*) has the energy and scope of an epic piece. In the most straightforward sense, it recounts the madcap adventures of Orpheus, the free-spirited narrator, as he searches the streets of Belgrade for the woman he loves (named Eurydice) and explores his artistic identity. The Orpheus of Greek mythology had the most beautiful voice in the world, so it's only fitting that John K. Cox's lively translation from Serbian conjures an Orpheus with a singular, seductive (and at times, wildly hilarious) voice of his own: "And there we were, climbing up slick steps, holding hands as lovers have done since time out of mind. Upstairs the glow from the streetlights overcame the gloom. The rain fluttered like a swarm of tiny insects around the chandelier. Our pale shadows quivered in the puddles on the shimmering asphalt." No matter which aspect of *The Attic*'s fantastical multi-genre story attracts you—the love story, the picaresque, the quest for self-understanding, the comical meta-critique of writing itself—Orpheus, like his mythological namesake, is an entrancing, haunting guide.
—*Ramona Demme*

Catherine Taylor
Apart
Brooklyn, NY: Ugly Duckling Presse, 2012

Documentary poetics can break your heart, and Catherine Taylor's first book of poems, *Apart*, certainly will. Part lyric essay, part verse memoir, the book explores the lasting impacts of apartheid in South Africa through archival research and, bravely, through family history, turning up startling images like "doodles of flowers and pretty little tea cups" in the margins of records of violence. Nothing is simple: "Everything outside is obscenely gorgeous" on the road to Robben Island. Taylor cautions that "the lyric's past seductions make a pretty mirror for the ugliness of corpses," but her assessment of identity, both national and familial, is inspirational and reminds us that "there's a gullet full of others to be loved including strangers."
—*Sarah Barber*

Natalie Peeterse
Black Birds: Blue Horse (An Elegy)
Los Angeles, CA: Gold Line Press, 2012

David St. John's selection for the 2011 Gold Line Press Poetry Chapbook Competition is an elegy by Natalie Peeterse for Nicole Dial, who was killed in Afghanistan while on a humanitarian mission. At this point in America's long war in Afghanistan and elsewhere, books such as *Black Birds: Blue Horse* serve to help elucidate the messy emotions and illogical business of war's cruelties. Peeterse masterfully guides readers through the fairly surreal sequence, manipulating white space and punctuation in a way that teaches us to read the poems. This is a sort of "poetry of witness," moving from Afghanistan to the streets of Washington, DC, examining "that cruel biology of the spirit" and searching for "things to cut the pain of waiting."
—*Paul-Victor Winters*

Jay Shearer
The Pulpit vs. The Hole
Los Angeles, CA: Gold Line Press, 2012

Selected by Percival Everett as winner of the 2011 Gold Line Press Fiction Chapbook Competition, Jay Shearer's long short story, *The Pulpit vs. The Hole*, is a coming-of-age tale replete with the finest ingredients for such a recipe: social awkwardness, sexual curiosity and its baggage, questions of familial identity, a sense of impending doom, religious guilt, and existential wonder. After a serious mishap, teenage Mennonite summer campers experience a strange sort of redemption. The boys from Cabin Six and a handful of interesting girls are first called "the Woodchucks," but because that's "gay," become "the Warlocks," because Warlocks "have actual *dark po*wers. Phenomenal Shit. Crazy Shit." Then, they become the more gender-inclusive "Wiccans." Shearer's teenage first-person narrator is strikingly spot-on, not overplayed or obstructive. What goes unanswered in the tale is as informative as the narrative itself, and we see these teenagers become aware of *something*, but still trapped in adolescence's awkward in-between. —*PVW*

Mark Hillringhouse
Between Frames / Poems and Photographs
Copenhagen, Denmark, and Florham Park, NJ: Serving House Books, 2012
Mark Hillringhouse uses a combination of dramatic black-and-white images and clear, terse language in his new book of poems and photographs. The poems, each accompanied by a photo, take us on a personal tour of Hillringhouse's New Jersey, "The aftermath of the city, that deep, red brick burning in the sun, the hush of cold dark rivers moving." I am struck by the sadness that seems to underlie the portraits in this book. The landscape Hillringhouse creates is present but forgotten, living and dying at the same time, inviting through the honest eye of a melancholic observer. I found myself traveling with him down the aisle of Woolworth's department store, sitting in the stands of a baseball game, riding in the front seat of his father's Buick Skylark, past Paterson and the Passaic River. In these familiar places I got to meet the people who inspired him—the poets, the photographers, the friends and family—and I came to recognize the things we are all forced to remember, the things that haunt us, the things we can't let go of. —*Kevin Carey*

Theresa Malphrus Welford, editor
The Cento: A Collection of Collage Poems
Pasadena, CA: Red Hen Press, 2011
The Cento is an anthology of poems that combine place, voice, and authorship to

carry the reader away from familiar beginnings. Most of the poems repurpose, rewrite, and reorganize an original document, whether it's a piece by a well-known poet or prose writer, Marvel comics, *New York Times* obituaries, grocery labels, or junk mail. This collection is a reminder of the many places where poems begin and the paths they can follow. Sharon Dolin's "Char'd Endings," a cento-sonnet using the closing lines of poems by Rene'Char, finishes:

> Keep us violent and friends to the bees on the horizon
> Such is the heart
> I hurt and am weightless

—*Chloé Yelena Miller*

Jill Osier
Bedful of Nebraskas
Buffalo, NY: Sunnyoutside, 2012

Bedful of Nebraskas, Jill Osier's new chapbook, expands in scope with each reading. Osier explores place, perspective, and loss with far-reaching resonance, probing the intersections of art and experience, light and dark, person and place, asking necessary, human questions about the role of the individual and the construction of meaning. In "One More Thing," Osier writes, "Then your dog dies, and the planets are more perfectly / imperfectly-shaped than ever. I'm not afraid? How else / explain invention?" Osier's work is suggestive and intimate, yet also of the world, populated with horses, cranberries, even elementary schools, and Osier works toward understanding tensions between the emotional and the concrete. As the speaker says in the title poem, "We give things names / to stop the spinning; we call it love / when we agree." —*Callista Buchen*

Micah Ling
Settlement
Buffalo, NY: Sunnyoutside, 2012

Micah Ling's *Settlement*, a two-act collection, explores conflict and colonialism in two contexts. The first half is about "The Reservations of the United States," and Act Two concentrates on "Palestinian Territories." Each section uses a unique assembled cast of voices and places (speakers include Marlon Brando, Bansky, and

Walid Husseini) to consider containment and opposition, as well as the cost to individual and community. Anger is a key force for the work. The collection begins with an epitaph from Sherman Alexie: "Poetry = Anger x Imagination." This resonates most strongly in pieces like the penultimate poem, a kind of list of definitions for "Settlement": "a coming to terms / ... / :Sinking of all or part of a structure. / ... / :Settlements settle the settlers." —CB

Jo Sarzotti
Mother Desert
Minneapolis: Graywolf Press, 2012

Jo Sarzotti's debut collection, *Mother Desert*, is composed of poems that reflect and then shatter the assumptions of the given world as "a lucky mirror, waiting / For the wrecking ball." Her voice is full of the assurance of the demolition expert who may not know what will be erected on the site but knows her job: to clear the way for something new—in this case, for the story of "The Girl with No Mother." These poems are balanced with a beautiful architecture—both within themselves and across the entire collection. The complex symbolism of the collection, exemplified by horses throughout, articulates a thematic progression that attempts to redeem the symbols themselves from the fate of being mere symbols. But it is the music of these poems that carries the reader along into this understanding, a language of the body, "Mute & sweaty / In the long last heave of homestretch." —*Michael T. Young*

Barbara Daniels
Quinn & Marie
Pueblo, CO: Casa de Cinco Hermanas Press, 2011

Barbara Daniels's most recent chapbook, *Quinn & Marie*, offers her readers the tightly crafted lyricism they have come to expect after 2008's *Rose Fever*, her first full-length volume. These new poems forge existential examinations—large and small—among the domestic lives of the two title characters. Quinn and Marie are, on one hand, kinds of Everyman characters, but distinct in their peculiarities. In "Harp," the initial lovemaking between the two is likened to swimming laps in a community pool and one worries that Quinn might drown. In "What They'll Lose," we see them "blunder toward each other, / eyes on each other's lips, / listening that way." By the end of the sequence of poems, we come to learn a bit about domestic togetherness, about how two might be able to listen "that way." —*PVW*

Lance Weller
Wilderness

New York: Bloomsbury, 2013

John Steinbeck wrote that a country has to experience war every twenty years so that each generation can know its horrors. Lance Weller's beautifully written novel *Wilderness* is as powerful an experience of war and battle—particularly the three-day 1864 Civil War Battle of the Wilderness—as this old peace-time soldier has ever read. The novel is not only about war and the effect it has on men and women; it is also about racism and the evil of the lack of compassion, as well as the power that caring can have on the trajectory of generations of people. —*Thomas E. Kennedy*

Contributors

Sarah Barber's poems (books 193) have appeared in *Poetry, Crab Orchard Review, The Journal, Fugue, Malahat*, and *FIELD*, among other places. Her book, *The Kissing Party*, was published in 2010.

Josh Billings (books 181) is a writer, translator and nursing student. He lives in Rockland, Maine.

Bruce Bond (poetry 63) is the author of eight books, most recently *The Visible, Peal*, and *Blind Rain*, which was a finalist for LSU's Poet's Prize in 2008. His tetralogy of new books entitled *Choir of the Wells* is forthcoming from Etruscan Press.

Melanie Braverman (poetry 124) is the author, most recently of *Red*. The work featured in this issue is from a book-length gesture in prose poems called *The World with Us in It*, others of which have appeared in *Poetry, American Poetry Review*, and *The Drunken Boat*.

Michael Broek's work (poetry 48) has appeared or is forthcoming in *The American Poetry Review, From the Fishouse, Blackbird, The Sycamore Review, The Cimarron Review*, and elsewhere. His chapbook, *The Logic of Yoo*, was issued by Beloit Poetry Journal in 2011.

Callista Buchen's (books 184, 195) poetry and prose have appeared in *Gigantic, Gargoyle, jmww, >kill author*, and others. Her reviews have been published in *Mid-American Review, The Collagist*, and *Prick of the Spindle*. She lives and teaches in Kansas.

Stephen Burt (poetry 127) is professor of English at Harvard. His third full-length book of poems, *Belmont*, will appear in spring 2013.

Drew Calvert (books 172) is a freelance writer based in Kuala Lumpur, Malaysia.

Kevin Carey (books 194) teaches writing at Salem State University. His new book of poems is *The One Fifteen to Penn Station*. He recently finished editing a documentary film about New Jersey poet Maria Mazziotti Gillan called *All That Lies Between Us*.

Ramona Demme (books 192) is an editorial assistant at Viking Press and lives in Brooklyn.

Alex Dimitrov (poetry 44) is the recipient of the Stanley Kunitz Prize for younger poets from *The American Poetry Review* and the founder of Wilde Boys, a queer poetry salon in New York City. His first collection, *Begging for It*, is forthcoming in 2013. His poems have appeared in *The Kenyon Review, Yale Review, Slate, Tin House*, and *Boston Review*.

Percival Everett ("Little Faith" 17) has written some books. If you write long enough, you win an award or two and so he has. He is professor of English at the University of Southern California.

Adam Felts ("Sam" 142) is a student at Emerson College in Boston, Massachusetts. He has a cat named Justice.

Dennis Hinrichsen's (poetry 88) most recent books are *Rip-tooth*, winner of the 2010 Tampa Poetry Prize, and *Kurosawa's Dog*, winner of the 2008 FIELD Poetry Prize. He lives in Lansing, Michigan.

Nathan Huffstutter's ("After I Smothered the Baby" 130) essays and reviews can be found online, where he is a regular contributor to *The Nervous Breakdown, The Collagist*, and *Emprise Review*.

Jeanne-Marie Jackson (books 187) teaches in the English Department at Connecticut College. Her writing has appeared in *Bookslut, Inside Higher Ed*, the *New Haven Review*, and *SLiPnet* in South Africa.

Laura Kasischke's (poetry 135) most recent poetry collection is *Space, in Chains*, which received the National Book Critics Circle Award as well as the Rilke Prize. She lives in Chelsea, Michigan, with her husband and son.

Thomas E. Kennedy's (books 197) 30+ books will include the forthcoming *Getting Lucky: New & Selected Stories, 1982–2012* and *Kerrigan in Copenhagen, A Love Story*, the third novel of his Copenhagen Quartet. Recent work has or will appear in *Boston Review, Ecotone, The Southern Review, American Poetry Review, New Letters*, and *Epoch*.

John King (books 189) is the host of the writing podcast *The Drunken Odyssey*. His work has appeared in *The Newer Yorker, Palooka, Gargoyle*, and others. While his doppelganger proudly teaches at the University of Central Florida, John resides at an undisclosed location and toils on his epic novel, *Guy Psycho and the Ziggurat of Shame*.

Aubrie Marrin's poems (9) have appeared in *Guernica, Harp & Altar, Sink Review, Colorado Review*, and elsewhere. She was a finalist for the 2012 Lexi Rudnitsky First Book Prize. She lives and works in Brooklyn.

Jynne Dilling Martin's poetry (67) has appeared in *Granta, The Kenyon Review, Ploughshares, Boston Review, New England Review, TriQuarterly, Southern Review,* and has been featured on the PBS *Newshour with Jim Lehrer.* She will be the 2013 Antarctica Artist in Residence.

Rachel May's writing ("Avery" 105) has been twice nominated for the Pushcart Prize, awarded the William Allen Creative Nonfiction Award, and published in *Indiana Review, Cream City Review, Meridian, Nimrod, Michigan Quarterly Review, Fugue,* and other journals.

Chloé Yelena Miller's (books 195) poetry chapbook, *Unrest,* is forthcoming from Finishing Line Press. Her work is published or forthcoming in *Alimentum, The Cortland Review, Narrative Magazine, Poet's Market,* and *Storyscape Literary Journal,* among others.

Susan White Norman ("Casco on the Foam Planet" 109) is a fiction writer and teacher living in Dallas, Texas. She is also the fiction editor of *Reunion: The Dallas Review.*

Donald Revell (poetry 14) is the author of eleven collections of poetry, most recently *The Bitter Withy* and *A Thief of Strings.* He has published five volumes of translations from the French, including Apollinaire's *Alcools,* Rimbaud's *Illuminations* and *A Season in Hell,* and Laforgue's *Last Verses.* His critical writings include *The Art of Attention* and *Invisible Green: Selected Prose.* Revell is a professor of English & creative writing at the University of Nevada, Las Vegas.

F. Daniel Rzicznek's (books 169) collections and chapbooks of poetry include *Vine River Hermitage, Divination Machine, Neck of the World,* and *Cloud Tablets.* Also coeditor of *The Rose Metal Press Field Guide to Prose Poetry: Contemporary Poets in Discussion and Practice,* Rzicznek teaches writing at Bowling Green State University in Ohio.

Will Schutt (poetry 156) is the author of the forthcoming book *Westerly,* winner of the 2012 Yale Series of Younger Poets competition. His poems and translations have appeared or are forthcoming in *Agni, FIELD, The New Republic,* and elsewhere.

Christine Sneed's ("The New, All-True CV" 70) stories have appeared in *Best American Short Stories, PEN/O. Henry Prize Stories, New Stories of the Midwest, Ploughshares,* and others. Her first book, *Portraits of a Few of the People I've Made Cry,* was a finalist for the *Los Angeles Times* Book Prize. Her second book, a novel titled *Little Known Facts,* will be out in early 2013.

Ben Stroud's ("Amy" 51) story collection *Byzantium* won the 2012 Bakeless Fiction Prize and will be published by Graywolf in 2013. His stories have appeared in *Electric Literature, One Story, Boston Review, Ecotone,* and other magazines.

Paul-Victor Winters (books 193) is a writer living in southern New Jersey. Recent poems have appeared or are forthcoming in *The New York Quarterly, Mead: The Magazine of Literature and Libations,* and *Scythe.*

Martha Witt (books 177) is the author of the novel *Broken As Things Are.* Her translations and short fiction are included in several national journals and anthologies. Her new translation of Pirandello's *Six Characters in Search of an Author,* will be published in 2014.

Marion Wyce (books 165) has received an AWP Intro Journals Award in Fiction and had her work performed in the Interact Theatre Company's stage series Writing Aloud.

Michael T. Young (books 196) has published three collections of poetry, most recently *Living in the Counterpoint*. His work has appeared or is forthcoming in *Edison Literary Review*, *Iodine Poetry Review*, *The Potomac Review*, *The Raintown Review*, and other journals and anthologies.

THE CHARLES ANGOFF FUND TO PAY WRITERS

The editors of *The Literary Review* would like to thank all of its contributors from the last volume year. This remarkable series of issues would not have been possible without you. As of this issue, TLR will be retiring the Charles Angoff Award for outstanding contributions during a volume year and establishing instead the Charles Angoff Fund To Pay Writers. Tax-deductible donations to our new fund can be made on the TLR website (www.theliteraryreview.org). Our goal is to begin distributing honorariums to every contributor by the end of 2013. We believe in supporting the arts by supporting our artists.

Ahmet Ada
Ellen Adams
Sherman Alexie
James Allardice
Kirstin Allio
Osama Alomar
Renée Ashley
Jesse Ball
Eric Barnes
Polina Barskova
Christian Barter
Barret Baumgart
Michael Bazzett
Miron Białoszewski
Daniel Blau
Paula Bomer
Bruce Bond
Steve Bradbury
Melanie Braverman
Michael Broek
Mark Budman
Stephen Burt
C.E. Cardiff
Alex Cigale
Cynthia Cruz
Joshua Diamond

Alex Dimitrov
Percival Everett
Adam Felts
D. Foy
David Georgi
Albert Goldbarth
Jeffrey Grinnell
James Grinwis
Micah Jon Heatwole
Derek Henderson
Margaret Hermes
Dennis Hinrichsen
H.L. Hix
John Hoppenthaler
Nathan Huffstutter
Laura Kasischke
Andrei Krasnyashykh
Joseph Levens
Bryon MacWilliams
Aubrie Marrin
Jynne Dilling Martin
Rachel May
Christian Nagle
Susan White Norman
Briandaniel Oglesby
Douglas J. Ogurek

Simon Perchik
Utz Rachowski
Molly Reid
Donald Revell
Judy Rowley
Juan Rulfo
C.J. Sage
Will Schutt
Christine Sneed
Aleš Šteger
Hilary Steinitz
Ian Stone
Ben Stroud
Cody Todd
Lee Upton
Joshua Weiner
Adam Wilson

Fiction Poetry Essays
Reviews Interviews Art

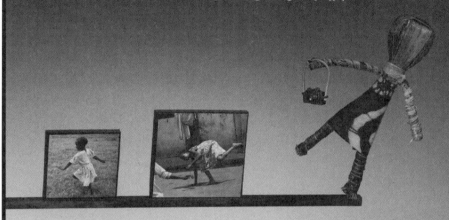

New Letters

www.newletters.org

University House/University of Missouri-Kansas City
5101 Rockhill Road, Kansas City, Missouri 64110
(816) 235-1168

Photos, sculpture, and banana-fiber doll design by Gloria Baker Feinstein.
Art photo by E. G. Shempf. From New Letters vol. 76 no. 3.

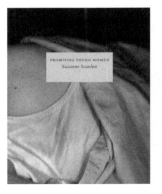

TLR

[hearts]

EMILY BOOKS

FACULTY
ELLEN AKINS
JEFFERY RENARD ALLEN
RENEE ASHLEY
REBECCA CHACE
WALTER CUMMINS
DAVID DANIEL
KATHLEEN GRABER
DAVID GRAND
H.L. HIX
THOMAS E. KENNEDY
MINNA PROCTOR
RENE STEINKE

GUEST ARTISTS

ALUMNI

WROXTON

WAMFEST

FDU IS HOME
TO THE LITERARY
REVIEW AND
THE WORDS AND
MUSIC FESTIVAL

Creative Writing at Fairleigh Dickinson University. BA and Low Residency MFA. Sessions in Madison New Jersey and Wroxton, England. Mentors, workshops, lectures, publishing, and good music. **www.fdu.edu/creativewriting**